Was Grandpa a Freeloader?

Civil War Pension Claims
North & South

Thomas Power Lowry M.D.

HISTORY BOOKS BY THE AUTHOR

The Story the Soldiers Wouldn't Tell

The Attack on Taranto

Tarnished Eagles

Civil War Bawdy Houses

Lincoln and Military Justice

Tarnished Scalpels (with Jack Welsh)

Swamp Doctor

VD and the Lewis & Clark Expedition

Confederate Heroines

Sexual Misbehavior in the Civil War

Mystery of the Bones (with P Willey)

Andersonville to Tahiti

Chinese Soldier in the Indian Wars

Confederate Death Sentences (with Lewis Laska)

Love & Lust: Intimate Civil War Letters

Merciful Lincoln

Utterly Useless Union Officers

Bad Doctors (with Terry Reimer)

Irish & German—Whiskey & Beer

Capital Courtesans

Civil War Rockets

Titanic Madness—Alzheimer's Caused?

Lost Lincolns

Civil War VD Hospitals

Thousand Stories You Don't Know

More Stories You Don't Know

WAS GRANDPA
A FREELOADER?

CIVIL WAR PENSION CLAIMS
NORTH & SOUTH

Thomas Power Lowry, MD

Idle Winter Press
Portland, Oregon

Idle Winter Press
Portland, Oregon
http://IdleWinter.com

This edition published 2016
Printed in the United States of America
The text of this book is in Alegreya

ISBN-13: 978-1945687006 (Idle Winter Press)
ISBN-10: 1945687002

CONTENTS

ACKNOWLEDGMENTS

The *Ur* source for thirteen of the author's books is the Civil War court-martial database created by Beverly A. Lowry—wife, companion, and consummate researcher. This 80,000 name source has aided dozens of other writers and will do so on into the future.

For matters Confederate, but most especially those pertaining to Robert E. Lee's immortal Army of Northern Virginia, Robert K. Krick has been, as ever, irreplaceable.

In the search for grave sites, census entries, and all matters of family history, I have been greatly aided by the wisdom and skill of the Rev. Dr. A. H. Ledoux.

When all else fails, I have once again called upon the patience and deep knowledge of the legendary and long-retired Michael P. Musick.

INTRODUCTION

Was Grandpa a Freeloader?

In 1912, at the age of sixty-six, my great-grandfather William H. Simms, a multimillionaire, applied for a Union Civil War veterans' pension. His application was approved. In the succeeding years, his pension check was increased twice. Why was a wealthy man receiving a government handout? And why was his wealthy widow still receiving Federal money when I was five years old?

At the peak of the pension madness, 37 percent of all Federal expenditures went to Union Civil War pensions. Much has been written about the roles of the Grand Army of the Republic and the Republican Party in this orgy of entitlement. Never before had the government spent so much on such a clearly defined group. How did this system evolve and who "deserved" such benefits? To answer these questions, we will examine the life of this grandpa, then the origins and evolution of the pension system, and, finally, draw together these strands in Simms' pension history.

William Henry Simms

The south, too, had Civil War pensions, but these were on a state by state basis. They will form a separate discussion.

William Henry Simms was born July 18, 1845 in Quainton, Buckinghamshire, England. His mother was widowed twice. She and William were living in poverty at Blissfield, Michigan when the war came. He was working as a common laborer in a broom handle factory and was allowed to sleep on the piles of sawdust. At age eighteen, he enlisted in Company L, First Michigan Engineers and Mechanics, and received a sixty- dollar bounty. He had blue eyes and stood five foot, four inches.

Over the next twelve months his regiment built bridges in the Murfreesboro, Tennessee, region including the celebrated Elk River Bridge near Pulaski, a wondrous pile of "beanpoles," erected not only in record time, but one that functioned perfectly.

They also repaired railroads, such as the Nashville and Chattanooga Railroad, and did a myriad of tasks, too small and too undramatic to be noted in the records.

On December 15, 1864, he was riding on a flatcar with several comrades and a pile of building material, when a hidden Confederate cannon swept the train. Simms was not wounded, escaped into the woods, and was soon surrounded. He smashed his musket and surrendered. The captors kicked him for disabling his weapon and also took his shoes. His next home was a Confederate prison camp at Meridian, Mississippi, a small facility with a barracks and a high fence. From there he was transferred to Andersonville.

Unlike 12,000 other Union prisoners, he did not die, but was exchanged April 1, 1865 and paroled April 28, 1865 at Jacksonville, Florida. A family story holds that on April 24, he was in line to board the *Sultana* as she lay at Vicksburg's levee, but was turned away because of overcrowding. While the dates don't match exactly, there was a large parole camp of paroled Andersonville prisoners at Vicksburg and hundreds of them died April 27, when her boilers exploded.

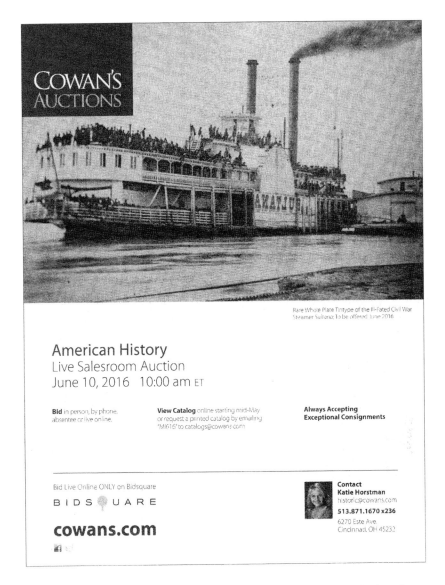

This rare whole plate tintype of the overloaded *Sultana* was offered for sale in June 2016 by Cowans.com.

His exact route home is unknown, but his official discharge date is June 24, 1865. (His descendants still possess a badly faded 18-inch square certificate making him a Life Member of the Illinois State Association of Union Prisoners of War.)

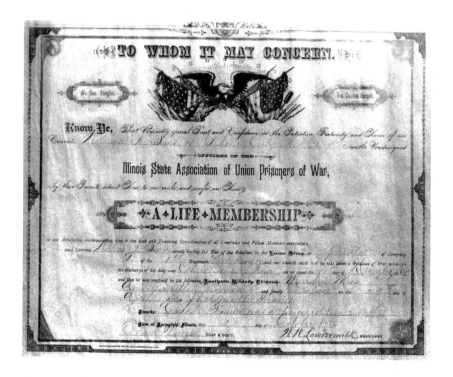

On returning home, he settled in Palmyra, Michigan, stayed there until 1871, and then moved to Gibson City, Illinois, where he spent the rest of his life. Relying again on family lore, he profited by using his mustering out money to buy lumber in tree-rich Michigan and ship it to treeless central Illinois, where new towns were springing up.

On August 30, 1877 the Rev. Samuel Lowe, at Gibson City, united William Simms with Emma Canterbury. She was not an ordinary 20-year old girl, but was the daughter of Asa and Margaret Canterbury, who in current dollars, were worth $340,000 in real estate and $75,000 in personal estates. During her wedding, Emma was attended by the other three of the locally-celebrated Canterbury Sisters: Chloe, Rosa, and Fanny. Whatever wealth may have come with his bride, William certainly did not squander it. Three years after their union, the 1880 census lists him as "grain dealer," reflecting his talent for buying farm land and improving it by laying drain tile, harvesting the crops, and re-investing the proceeds. As he prospered he indulged in such frivolity as chartering an entire railroad car, to take his friends to see the Chicago Cubs. A postcard published around 1900 by "J. M. Freeland, druggist" shows the "residence of W. H. Simms," an elegant Victorian confection, said to be the first in town with running hot water.

Simms not only improved land and raised corn, but his production was such as to justify a canning operation. One brand was marketed as "Pony Brand Sugar Corn." The little boy on the pony was the author's great-uncle, William H. Simms, Jr., recalled in fond memory as "Uncle Bill," who carved the turkey at Christmas.

William and Emma produced four children: Nellie, who died at age four; an unnamed boy who died very young; William, Jr., and Chloe, the author's grandmother.

Here we see Emma Canterbury Simms in her Victorian finery, probably a leading light in the small town society of Gibson City, Illinois.

The family continued to prosper. The 1900 census shows the household with Mary Regan, a 20-year old live-in servant, born in Ireland. William grew four inches from his enlistment height. Chloe went on to marry Russell Lowry, a successful San Francisco banker.

Chloe Simms, seen here as a young woman, attended a finishing school in Washington, DC. In her later years she devoted herself to generously funding the First Christian Church of Oakland, California, and to reading each monthly issue of the *Readers Digest*.

William, Jr. served in the Army in World War I, was gassed in the trenches, survived, and went on to a career in the insurance industry. The senior William Simms, a skinny malnourished youth, a graduate of Andersonville, grew rotund with prosperity.

As it comes to all of us, death visited William H. Simms August 4, 1918. The cause? Cerebromalacia, "softening of the cerebrum." His very long, hand-written, and detailed probate record began, "First, I give and bequest to my Wife Emma C. Simms, One Thousand Dollars, to be paid to her by any Executors herein after named, upon my death ... I also give and devise to my wife, Emma C. Simms, our present home with all the furniture, furnishings and belongings thereto, upon and including Lots fourteen and fifteen in Block thirty in First Addition to Gibson ... I also give and bequest to my wife ... the Northwest Quarter of Section Four in Township Twenty-three North Range Seven east of Third P.M." There follows a long series of bequests, including those to Chloe and William, Jr, all couched in the somewhat arcane jargon of professional surveyors.

His probate records, printed from digitized online records, are hard to read, but with patience and considerable magnification, a remarkable collection of properties and investments emerges.

Reducing these items to everyday language, the Illinois farmlands, the California vineyards, and the San Diego real estate, would be worth roughly $31 million in today's dollars.

Record of the Last Will and Testament

STATE OF ILLINOIS, } ss.
FORD COUNTY.

[faded handwritten probate record]

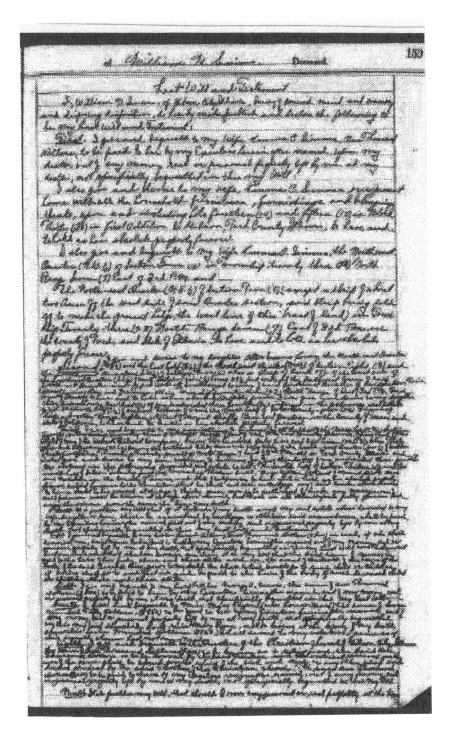

CHAPTER 1
THE UNION PENSION SYSTEM

The pension issue did not exist in a vacuum, separate from the nation's history. It is one piece in the great jumbled panorama of a historic turning point. A Procrustean simplification can identify at least nine salient and intertwined issues.

There is the transformation of America from a rural nation into a whole new framework of mechanized agriculture, a rapidly expanding network of railroads, an efficient system of mass-produced goods, and an era of high finance, sometimes vital, but often under the thumbs of the Robber Barons such as Jay Gould and John D. Rockefeller. In all these developments, the North moved far ahead of the wounded South.

Then there was the carefully watched American experiment in democracy. Nearly all the rest of the world was still ruled by strong men (and of course, Queen Victoria), a smorgasbord of kings, emperors, and czars, most of whom doubted the viability of a representational form of government. To their surprise, the United States did not collapse but emerged even stronger than before. Riven by Civil War bitterness, yes, but still thriving and growing, with a powerful iron and coal industry and an abundance of wheat, enough to make wealthy the grain exporting merchants of New York, such as William Henry Power, another of the author's great-grandparents. (He paid for a substitute to avoid Union service).

Yet another turning point marked the war. *Ante bellum* the nation's clergy was more ecclesiastical than political, unlike most other nations, where church and state were conjoined twins. Victoria was Defender of the Faith, that faith being the Church of England, Henry VIII's gift to Christianity. The kings of Spain were titled His Most Catholic Majesty. The czars of Russia were for centuries in the dark embrace of the Orthodox Church, a symbiosis now resurrected by Vladimir Putin. Church and state fusion lives on in the Islamic Republic of Iran and the Islamic Republic of Pakistan. But here in the United States, in no small part a legacy of Thomas Jefferson, we are a secular nation. But in the pre-war years, and even more so during the years 1861-1865, the churches divided into North and South. The former tended to designate slavery as an abomination, while their counterparts, in a thousand sermons, declared slavery to be ordained of God.

The great conflict was enhanced a deep current of irony. The South was obsessed by states' rights. (Confederate General

States Rights Gist [his actual name] was killed at the Battle of Franklin.) The insistence on these rights inhibited the Confederacy's ability to impose coherence and cooperation in such areas as troop allocation and railroad schedules. The war also left the residue of a far more powerful central government, the very outcome that the secessionists dreaded most.

The 1865 Grand Review, in which 150,000 Union soldiers marched through Washington, DC, astounded some European observers. These armed and battle-hardened men did not attempt a *coup d'état*. They were a people's army. Not like the misnamed forces of the Democratic Republic of North Korea, which is neither democratic nor a republic, but an actual people's army. There was no cabal of colonels plotting a takeover and a military junta. The Union Army's volunteer officers were teachers, bankers, businessmen, engineers, local politicians. Very few saw themselves as career officers. Though civilians at heart, they had through years of bloody combat, become competent killers. Yet their goal was not more gore and conflict, but a return to home, family, church, and work. Unlike Aladdin's genie, which could not be stuffed back in the bottle, this huge army with its legions of suppliers could be made to disappear. In a puff of smoke, it vanished, leaving a very reduced regular army, and a few resentful volunteer troops kept on out of necessity.

The final two threads in this exposition, both relevant to the subject of pensions are: (1) self-identity, and (2) the rise of special interest groups. Regarding the former, most Americans before the war were Jeffersonian in spirit. They favored manliness, personal independence and self-reliance, and were opposed to strong central government. They did not like being told what to do or how to worship. They were yeoman farmers, the plain folk, the salt of the earth. They believed fervently in local civic virtues, in voting, in a free press, and in severing the link between church and state.

They regarded the central government as a dangerous necessity, to be watched eternally, lest its powers increase. "I ask little of it; it should ask little of me." In contemporary affairs we see it in Greta Garbo's "I want to be alone," and the Hollywood action heroes with their "I work alone." An early 18th century prototype might be Daniel Boone, who tamed the wilderness with flintlock and ax. He had no entourage of civic affairs advisers. And whatever mixture of myth and reality adheres to Boone, he seems Jeffersonian to the bone.

Here the background music shifts to a minor key, the time-honored cinematic way of ushering in a darker or contrary theme. At the 1865 Grand Review a banner hung from the Capitol itself: "The only national debt we can never pay is the debt we owe the victorious Union Soldiers." Was this the opening salvo in a conflict between the Jeffersonian ideal and a sense of entitlement that would swell in the coming decades? As the future brought ever-increasing entitlements, it also spawned a whole industry of critics, who saw the increasingly politicized veterans as moochers with hands out, palm up, "Sucking off the government teat," as one observer put it.

Pari passu with the rise of a sense of entitlement was an effloresce of special interest groups and lobbyists. Today, they are legion. They tread the halls of Congress. They picket the steps of the Supreme Court. They fund PACs under wildly misleading names. They inflame the listeners of talk radio shows and fill Internet inboxes with dire warnings. There are literally hundreds of such special interests. A moments reflection will bring forth a dozen. The American Association of Retired Persons. The National Rifle Association. The National Association for the Advancement of Colored People. The Sons of Confederate Veterans. The American Legion. The Pharmaceutical Manufacturers Association. The American Petroleum Institute. The American Medical Association. The American Civil Liberties Union.

In the 19th century the largest and most effective lobby group was the Grand Army of the Republic, with its close links to the Republican Party.

"To care for him who shall have borne the battle, and for his widow, and his orphan." With these words, in his Second Inaugural Address, Abraham Lincoln foreshadowed a pension system which was to grow beyond anyone's imagining. The first formalization of the wish to aid veterans was passed by Congress in 1862. It provided pensions for Union army soldiers who had suffered permanent bodily injury as a direct result of military service. The monthly payments ranged from $8 (for privates) to $30 for upper grade officers. The pension would begin only if the veteran filed his claim within one year of the date of his discharge. In the following forty years, as the nation changed, and the veteran's organizations, especially the Grand Army of the Republic (GAR), gained influence, two men would play a major role. Though forgotten now, they bestrode the

Victorian Age like colossi. The first was George E. Lemon. He was a captain in the 125th New York Infantry, taken prisoner and paroled at Harpers Ferry, and wounded at Bristoe Station. In 1877, he began publishing the *National Tribune*, a newspaper devoted to the welfare and benefits of the Union veterans. It came out monthly 1877-1881 and weekly 1882-1917. At its prime the *Tribune* had 250,000 paid subscribers. In it, Lemon argued decade after decade for increased veterans' benefits. An enormous marble tombstone marks his resting place at Section U, Lot 18, Rock Creek Cemetery, Washington, DC.

The other colossus was John A. "Black Jack" Logan. Today, four counties are named after him; an enormous equestrian statue graces Logan Circle in Washington, DC.

Logan served in the Mexican War and was a Union major general in the Civil War. He was a vigorous son of Illinois, serving in the state senate, then as a congressman and finally a US senator. (Logan was no civil rights champion. In 1853 he helped pass a law prohibiting any African American from settling in Illinois.) He led the fight to make Memorial Day a national holiday and, while serving as the second Commander-in-Chief of the GAR, promoted the interests of veterans both in legislation and by his wildly popular style of oratory, both passionate and forceful, nicknamed "spread eagle" speaking. In the election of 1884 Logan ran as James G. Blaine's vice-president, in their failed bid at the White House. Logan died two years later, and now rests in an elaborate granite mausoleum at the National Soldiers Home cemetery.

The GAR was many things in many places during its years. It was both a national organization and a vast network of "lodges" with varying membership requirements and rituals. The individual groups tended to resemble the local cultures.

There were lodges of relatively wealthy men and lodges of the less well off. The vast majority of members were native-born. The GAR had little interest in the immigrants who had served in the Union army or in the 240,000 African American's who had also served in uniform.

Pensions meant different things to different people. To some the breakdown of local communities and neighborhoods meant the erosion of help for those fallen on hard times. There must be some larger body to provide succor, in this case the government. Critics opined that wealthy veterans had no need for pensions while those in poverty were there because of their own shiftless and dissolute ways. Supporters of pensions, including such inflammatory agents as George E. Lemon, saw military service as creating a debt which could never be fully paid, and opposition to pensions as dastardly betrayal of the nation's moral obligations.

The evolution of the pension system would fill books, and has, but the crucial turnings points are four in number. In 1862 the requirements for a pension were simple: proof of honorable military service and a service-connected disability. A major shift came with the Arrears Act of 1879. Under this new act, the disability still had to be service-connected, but proof of service could be not only military records, but also affidavits by comrades. ("Yes, I remember old George; he was in my company.") But more dramatic was the ability to claim back-dated benefits. Imagine a man discharged in 1865 who in 1875 filed a claim. If it was approved, he would receive payments not only forward from 1875 but also payment for the years 1865-1875.

Pension Commissioner John E. Bentley described the new guidelines as "an open door...for the perpetuation of fraud." The possibility of sudden (relative) wealth, galvanized many veterans, but the true motive force was an army of pension agents and pension attorneys, who, in a carnival of greed and opportunism, stood to gain a fee of $10 for each successful new claim, $200 in today's money.

The year 1890 brought another major change, the Dependent and Disability Act, which granted pensions to all veterans who had served at least ninety days, were honorably discharged, and were currently unable to perform manual labor. (The author's experience as a disability evaluator for the California Workers' Compensation system exposed him to a parade of doubtful spasms, limps, and aching backs.) This new act removed the necessity of being service-connected and required no need for economic necessity. A wealthy businessman who never lifted anything heavier than a pen was as entitled as a quarryman. The final event in this progression came with President Theodore Roosevelt's executive order of 1904, making all veterans over the age of 62 eligible for pensions; old age itself was now a disability.

An extreme example of the durability of the pension industry is that of Irene Triplett whose visage (courtesy of the *Wall Street Journal*) graces the back cover of this book. At the time of this writing she was still drawing a Union Civil War pension. Her father, Moses Triplett, was sixteen when the war began. He first served in two Confederate regiments, the 53rd North Carolina Infantry and the 26th North Carolina Infantry. On the march to Gettysburg, Moses deserted and enlisted August 1, 1864 in a Union regiment, the 3rd North Carolina Mounted Infantry. He received an honorable discharge after a year of service. In 1885 he applied for and received a pension. His first wife, Mary, died childless. In 1924 he married Elida Hall, 49 years his junior. Such May-December marriages were not rare. The woman, usually desperately poor, received some financial security while the man got care in his old age. It was not a happy match. The couple had three babies who died young. Irene was born in 1930 when her father was age 83 and her mother was 34. Both Elida and Irene had severe psychiatric problems and were unable to fend for themselves when Moses died. Both resided for years in the county poor house. Elida died in 1967. Irene now lives in a skilled nursing home. They lived hard lives, in hard times, in a hard part of the country. Irene recalls becoming addicted to tobacco in the first grade and of being beaten severely both in school and at home. There is no record of illiterate and irascible Moses joining the GAR.

Another example of whether a soldier "deserved" his pension is George Washington Stogdale. He originally served in Company A of the 52nd Virginia Infantry, Confederate of course. He was captured and sent to the prisoner of war camp at Point Lookout. There, in October 1864, he volunteered for Union service and was assigned to Company A, 4th US Volunteers. Five months after enlisting he was in the Benton Barracks Hospital, near St. Louis, Missouri, disabled with gonorrhea. After three months of treatment he was still too sick for duty and was "discharged for disability." In 1895 he applied for, and received, a

Union pension. Upon his death in 1910, Stogdale's widow began receiving a pension.

A more clearly deserving Union soldier was Pvt. Jacob Miller, Company K, 9th Indiana Infantry. At Chickamauga, he was shot between the eyes, damaging both his skull and, apparently, part of his brain and left optic nerve. He did not wish to be taken prisoner, so he managed to stagger, half-conscious, to medical help. A series of Union doctors refused to operate on him, fearing it might kill him. After several months, he went AWOL to his home town, where two civilian doctors removed a musket ball from the hole in his forehead. Seventeen years after his wound a buckshot fell out. Thirty-one years later two pieces of lead fell out. He lived a total of sixty-four years after that day at Chickamauga, always in pain and lacking sight in his left eye. His application for a disability pension is dated September 22, 1864.

Simms was clearly a GAR member. The records of Lott GAR Post 70, of Gibson City, are still in the manuscripts of the Abraham Lincoln Presidential Library in Springfield. Although the records are not complete, he was post adjutant in 1880, a dues-paying member for the next eleven years, and post commander in 1891. He soon met Teddy Roosevelt's criterion for a pension—being age 62 or older. At age sixty-six, in August 1907, Simms applied for a pension "under the Act of February 6, 1907." In August 1915, he requested an increase in his pension. "I am ... entitled to the raise for being 70 years of age and I make this application under the provisions of the Act of May 11, 1912." His pension was raised to $20 a month, which continued until his death on August 4, 1918.

Six weeks later, his wealthy widow, Emma Canterbury Simms, applied for and received a pension of $25 a month, which continued until her death February 19, 1937, a time when the author was in kindergarten at Frank C. Havens Elementary School.

Was the Civil War pension system a vast fraud? Certainly one can argue that it was driven by politicking and by over-eager pension attorneys. But the laws and their application were the creation of a representational form of government and at some level must represent the will of the people. One of the most dedicated students of this issue is Professor Theda Skocpol. In her book *Protecting Soldiers and Mothers* (Harvard University Press, 1992) she concluded, "After poring over Annual Reports of Commissioners of Pensions to find any possible systematic statistics, I have reluctantly concluded that nothing exact can be said about the proportions of illegitimate pensioners or expenditures."

CHAPTER 2
NOT JUST WORDS

The issues of both Confederate and Union pensions have left us a great ocean of written words: the records of military service, physicians' certificates, comrades' affidavits, court clerks' approvals. The enabling legislation fills pages of tightly spaced legal jargon. Designating words flow like rivers. "Partial." "Total." "Both eyes." "One foot." "Artificial limb." "Wartime widow." "Post-war Widow." "Both hands." "One eye." "Disability." The actuality of the wounds pale behind this sandstorm of paperwork.

The old veterans are long gone. What we have are records. And photographs. In the century before Photoshop and other image manipulation programs the camera usually told the truth. And that truth is intense, shocking, and often horrifying. These photographs, mostly from Union sources, are equally valid for the shattered Sons of the South. Every war produces immeasurable suffering. Every war creates ghastly wounds. So too, the Civil War.

Our discussions and portrayals of the Civil War today are deeply flawed. Authors and enthusiasts nitpick the decisions of long dead generals. Writers walk the fields of old battles seeking authenticity. But today, as he strolls the rolling hills and the shady creek beds, the fields of fire are not obscured by clouds of acrid smoke. Today, the seeker does not need to hop over mounds of corpses. Today the seeker is not distracted by the sounds of musket balls ripping the air by his head, nor is he startled by the screams of the wounded. Screaming is not popular with Civil War audiences. None of the widely-viewed Civil War movies have screaming. The wounded fall down quietly. When the cameras stop rolling, they get up and walk away, but 150 years ago a man shot through the pancreas will feel the released juices digesting him inside, with a deep boring pain. He will claw his uniform open, hoping that a hand upon his belly will stop the agony. His nearby comrade, with a musket ball through his femur, totally unable to stand, will feel the torn periosteum send its messages of agony up to his brain. The man in the following line has taken a musket ball though his bladder, and curls up on the ground, hoping somehow this posture will lessen the sensation of the salty acid urine searing his guts and pelvic muscles. None of these men, or others like them scattered here and there across the fields of glory, are thinking of national issues or political slogans. They are each in their closed personal universes, with their only companion the all-encompassing pain, so blind and deaf to the rest of the world that they are not even aware of their own screams.

But these attempts to put suffering into words are, once again, mere words. And the photographs? They speak for themselves.

A. J. Hutchins,
Co. K, 25th Ohio Vols.

Wm. H. McFarland,
Co. B, 5th Wisconsin Vols.

V. N. Higgins,
Co. H, 2nd Me. Vols.

Thomas Shields,
Co. G, 62nd N.Y. Vols.

S. M. Dyer,
Co. I, 5th Wis. Vols.

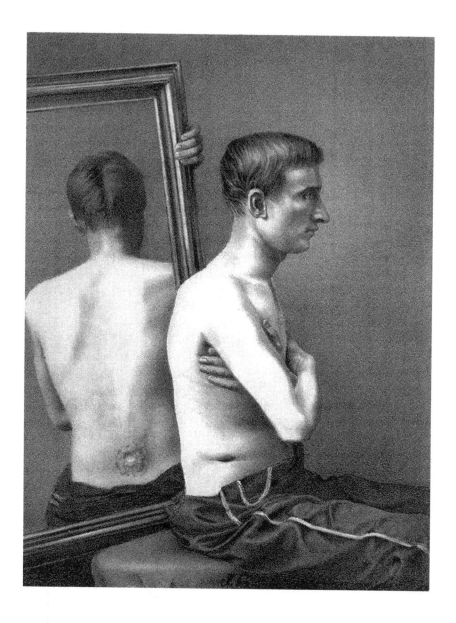

AMPUTATION of 3d 4th & 5th METACARPALS
Pvt Robt Fryer Co. G. 52 N.Y.

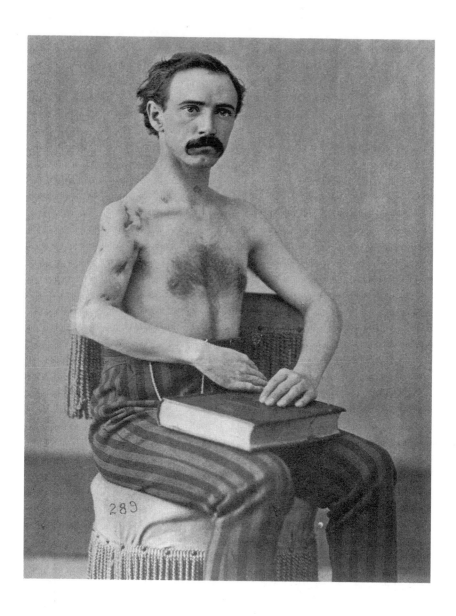

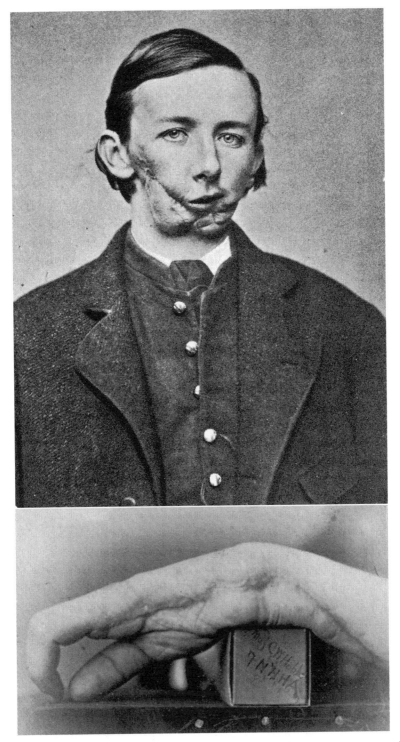

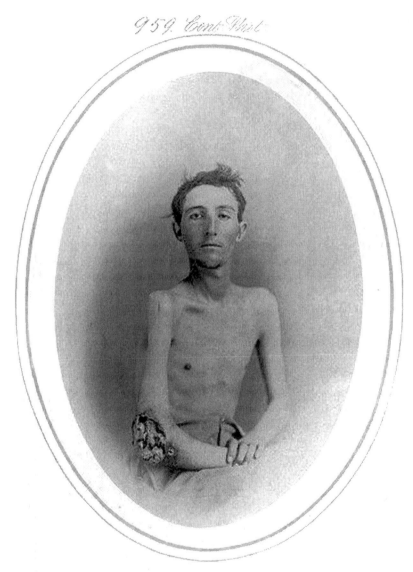

GUNSHOT FRACTURE OF ELBOW JOINT
Gangrenous condition of wound
Pvt. James H. Stokes Co. K. 185 NY

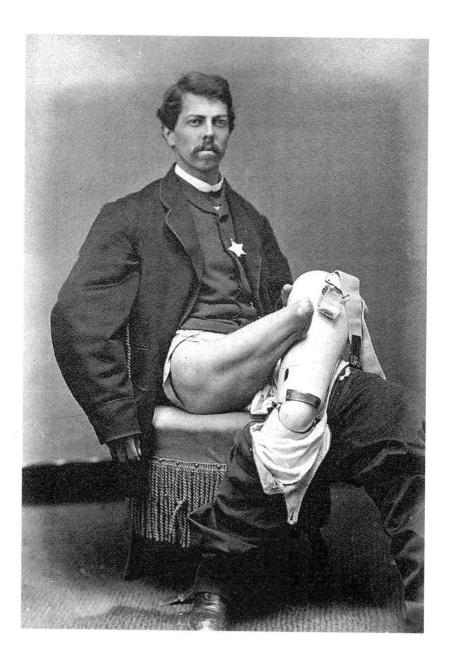

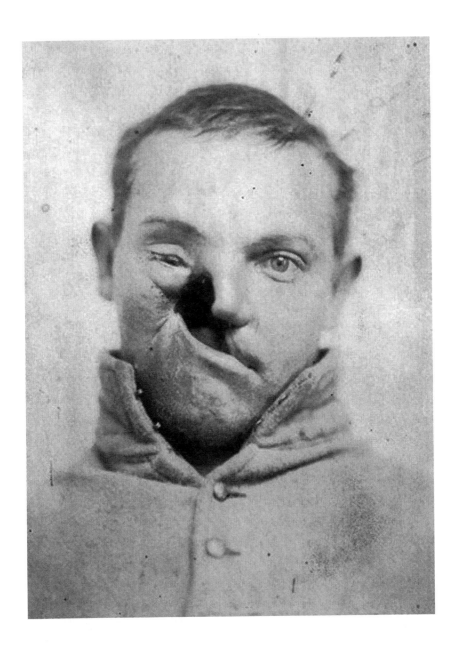

CHAPTER 3
CONFEDERATE PENSIONS

The Confederate government ceased to exist in April 1865, so could provide no pensions. Such pensions were therefore on a state by state basis. Each state had its own problems and policies. Such pensions as existed were often begun many years after the war and limited to clearly service-connected injuries. As the decades passed, the terms became more liberal. Finally, a few border states, which had stayed with the Union, issued pen-sions to Confederate. And as the last few veterans faded away, the United States Congress pensioned Confederate veterans.

Fourteen states issued pensions to Confederate veterans. Here are those states and the years they began paying pensions. Alabama (1867). Arkansas (1891). Florida (1885). Georgia (1870).

Kentucky (1912). Louisiana (1898). Missouri (1911). Mississippi (1888). North Carolina (1867). Oklahoma (1915). South Carolina (1887). Tennessee (1891). Texas (1889). Virginia (1867).

For purposes of this essay, the author has chosen to focus on just one Confederate state: Virginia. This is for at least three reasons. First, it is the author's current choice of domicile. Second, its Confederate pension records are online, through the Library of Virginia. Third, the availability of Mark E. Rodgers' magisterial *Tracing the Civil War Veteran Pension System in the State of Virginia* (The Edwin Mellen Press, Queenston, Ontario, 1999).

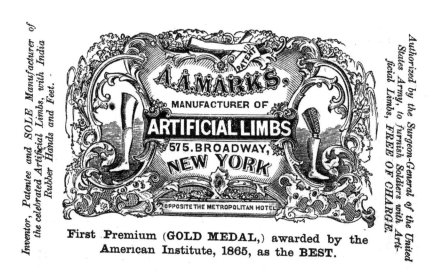

First Premium (**GOLD MEDAL,**) awarded by the American Institute, 1865, as the **BEST**.

By the time the guns fell silent, the State of Virginia had thousands of shattered veterans and neither the money nor a coherent policy for relieving their misery There was no succor coming from the North; the Union had its hands full with its own pension system, nor was their much Northern public opinion favoring aid to the states which had just attempted to destroy the Union. The first efforts of the General Assembly were directed solely to providing artificial limbs. Between 1867 and 1870 the state provided 330 artificial limbs, at a cost of $40,000 ($1.2 million in today's money).

There were artificial limb factories both North and South. Documentation and promotional material is more easily located for the Northern facilities.

In 1875, the state began to phase out the direct provision of artificial limbs in favor of "commutation," in which the wounded veteran received money, which was his to spend on medical care, prostheses, and whatever else that best suited his needs. In 1882, the General Assembly provided commutation to "such maimed soldiers, sailors, and marines in lieu of artificial limbs or eyes ... as may not heretofore received the same under the provisions of former acts." The Act of 1884 laid out in greater detail (see Appendix A) the requirements for application, including medical certificates and details about where and how the wound occurred and under whose command.

In 1888, there was a major restructuring of the entire program, which became a pension system, with annual payments, to be made each April to qualified applicants. By this time the United Confederate Veterans and the United Daughters of the Confederacy had become influential lobbying organizations, which may account for the newly created benefits for widows. Four factors might disqualify an applicant: a personal income of over $300 per year; personal property valued at over $1,000; receipt of a pension from any other state or from the United States; and being a resident in a soldier's home. Virginia was still mostly rural and used hand labor; there far fewer clerks and teachers, hence the extent of a disability was usually couched in "inability to perform manual labor." The wound must have been incurred while in military service. Soldiers who has lost one leg, one foot, one arm, one eye, or one hand received $30 per year. Those who lost two eyes, two feet, two hands, or a foot and a hand received $60. Partial disability, as described by a physician, brought the soldier $15 each April.

Under the 1888 law, a widow would receive $30 a year if her husband had been killed in service, and if she had not re-married, and if she lived in Virginia, and if her income was under $300 a year, and if her personal property was worth less than $1,000, and if she was not receiving any other kind of pension.

1898 brought innovations. The auditor was instructed to create a roster of all Confederate veterans living in Virginia. The 1898 law created a home for Confederate widows and the sisters and daughters of dead Confederate soldiers. Those who had lost two limbs or both eyes had their annual check increased by $40, the same amount now to be received by widows who had not re-married. Many personal bills were introduced in the Virginia legislature, creating pensions for specific individuals. The *Confederate Veteran* magazine, published 1893-1932, carried frequent articles and editorials advocating increased veterans' benefits.

In 1900 came more changes. Veterans whose disabilities occurred after the war were added, as were widows whose veteran husbands died after the war. Widows' applications were both vetted and promoted by the United Daughters of the Confederacy. Men who had lost an arm, or a foot, or a leg, or a hand during the war had their annual check increased to $50. Those who had lost both eyes, both feet, both hands, and a hand and a foot were increased to $100 a year. Those disabled by age were now eligible. Widows who had lost husbands during the war had their checks increased to $40, while those who lost husbands after the war received $25. The same property exclusions remained in place.

As the new century moved on, the legislators seemed increasingly concerned that fraudsters and imposters might be imposing on the taxpayers of Virginia. One leading student of the Army of Northern Virginia, wrote, "These old gummers would get together. and swear for each other. George would 'remember' that Bob served next to him in Capt. Webster's Company. A few weeks later Bob would do the same for George." The 1902 regulations included these changes: The applicant had to be a Virginia resident for two years prior to applying and a resident of his current county for a full year. The new law created six classes of applicants. A. Those who had lost two eyes, two feet, two hands, or a hand plus a foot, from wounds or related surgical procedures, were increased to $100 per year. B. Those who had lost one arm, one leg, one foot, or one hand were increased to $50 per year. C. Those who had not lost a limb, but were disabled by wounds or disease were increased to $30 a year if totally disabled or $15 per year if partially disabled. D. Those age 65 and older, with faithful service (no desertions), who were disabled by age received $30 if totally disabled and $15 if partially disabled. E. Every unmarried widow whose husband died during the war received $40. F. Every unmarried widow whose husband had served faithfully but died <u>after</u> the war received $25.

The 1902 act also tightened many requirements. Now those with only $150 or less annual income could qualify. The personal property limit was reduced from $1,000 to $500. Any man in a veterans' home was excluded. The required documentation was increased. Two comrades must swear that they knew him in service. If he had died, there must be a formal death certificate signed by a physician. The War Department records must show no dereliction of duty, and all those who received benefits under the 1900 law had to be re-certified. Now, for the first time, there were legal penalties for submitting false information: up to a year in jail, a $100 fine, or both. Also for the first time benefits were totally denied to anyone who had ever deserted, or to widows who had divorced their husband, or to substitutes, or to the widows of substitutes.

In 1906, the Virginia legislature added further restrictions. The veteran must have been a Virginia resident before April 1, 1861, and any widow, to be eligible, had to be a Virginia resident since 1899. In 1908 there were further changes, which both loosened and tightened various aspects on the pension program. All persons receiving benefits received a 50 percent increase in their annual check. Veterans of other Confederate states could receive Virginia benefits, but only if their home state reciprocated with Virginia. Veterans over age eighty could have personal property of $1,500 and still receive benefits. The tightened provisions reflect concern about fraud under the 1900 law. All those who benefited under that law had to file new, complete applications, with all the required documentation, and were receive no benefits until they had submitted the new required papers.

The calendar marched on. The old got older. The sick got sicker. In 1910, over 2,300 veterans received no money because the state funds were running dry. The legislature passed a one-time emergency appropriation of $65,000. In 1911, money was still short; all benefits were cut 10 percent. The following year, the 10 percent was replaced, and the state authorized the counties to levy taxes for veterans' benefits. (Until 1912 all benefits had been paid from the state general fund.) A further provision gave $40 annually to women who had served at least 12 months as matrons (nurses) in Confederate hospitals.

In 1914 money was added for Confederate widows not yet on the pension rolls. The United Daughters of the Confederacy continued to have a strong hand in determining which widows qualified. The legislature also set aside $3,000 for veterans excluded from soldiers' homes because of cancer or contagious disease. A personal bill awarded $50 to Richard Snow for identifying fraudulent claims in Greene County. In 1918, widows whose husbands died after the war began to receive the same benefits as those whose husbands had died during the war, and benefits could be paid to those widows who had remarried. In 1920, each county was ordered to count and list all living veterans in that county, including name, age, postal address, value of property, and any income. In 1922, the counties were ordered to gather even more information: each veteran's service, including rank, company, regiment, and time of service, and send copies of these rosters to the State Librarian. Apparently the economy was picking up: all Civil War benefits were increased 50 percent. (This may have only covered inflation.)

A new era was dawning. In the halls of the capitol, in newspaper editorials, in the veterans' publications, there was talk of asking the Federal government (the Yankees!) to fund the benefits of the Confederate veterans. Some said it would be a stain on Virginia's honor to beg for Northern money. Others said, in essence, "We are all Americans again. Why not ask?" In a remarkable change, the Virginia legislature authorized $25 pensions for "loyal" blacks who had served the Virginia troops. The thousands of black women who had nursed the sick and wounded got...nothing. An increasing trend was reflected in a 1924 law which awards widow's benefits only if she had married the veteran before December 31, 1882. There had been many June-December marriages, old veterans marrying very young girls. He got nursing care, and perhaps some romance, in his dotage. She, usually illiterate and desperately poor, got a roof over her head and some reliable income. A 1926 act provided money to establish a home for the needy widows, sisters, and daughters of Virginia veterans.

Hamlet mused, "What dreams may come when we have shuffled off this mortal coil?" (3.1.56). And indeed, Virginia veterans were shuffling off at a great rate. In 1928, there were only 2,300 still alive. In 1931, the Sons of Confederate Veterans surveyed the entire South. They found that 1,300 Virginia veterans were receiving $30 a month, while 4,100 widows got checks of $10 per month. Virginia, like every state, was hit hard by the

Great Depression. All pensions were cut by 30 percent, creating cries of outrage from both the United Daughters of the Confederacy and the Sons of Confederacy. From 1933 to 1945, there were few changes, mostly slight increases in benefits. In 1958, the United States Congress voted to take over benefit payments to all Confederate veterans and their widows.

(Virginia's largess must be seen in context. In 1910, the average Confederate veteran across the South received a check for $47.24. Those in the Old Dominion received $23.38.)

It was time to end the show. Since the Civil War, there had been the Spanish-American War, the First World War, the Second World War, the Korean War, and the Viet Nam war. The Cold War still raged. Medicare, Medicaid, and Social Security provided benefits undreamed of in decades past. The Virginia Civil War pension system had served its purpose. It was over. Finished. Done. In 1978, Virginia ceased all Civil War pensions.

CHAPTER 4

THE CLASS OF '88

After the Virginia legislature passed the revised pension laws of 1888, a total of 5,590 veterans applied for pensions under provisions of that act. The intrepid researcher Mark E. Rodgers spent hundreds of hours in the Library of Virginia, reading every one of these applications and reducing each to a summary, the summaries arranged in alphabetical order, and presented in his book, *Tracing the Civil War Veteran Pension System in the State of Virginia*. A whole sheaf of papers might be condensed into a brief paragraph, as shown in this example from page 564 of the book. "Wills, Henry Bedford County 58th VA Infantry Co. A Wounded in action. 1864 Winchester, VA. Gunshot wound of neck and right shoulder. 1888 Application approved $15.00."

The Library of Virginia has since digitized these records and they are available online. In life, there always seems to be a trade-off. Rodgers had the advantage of handling the original papers, with the best chance of interpreting the sometimes difficult handwriting. He had the disadvantage of the time and money needed for his long days in the library. The current researcher has the luxury of connecting with the library over the Internet from the comfort of home, but he suffers a disadvantage if the digitization process has led to the pixilation that bedevils so many online records. Presented hereinafter are a dozen sample applications, together with the Compiled Military Service Records of each man.

Willis Wills, age 27, a schoolmaster, was enlisted in Company G (Capt. Thomas M. Boyd's Company), 19th Va. Infantry, on May 1, 1861, and enrolled at Massie's Mill. In August 1861 he is described as absent sick at Centreville. In October 1861 he is still in the hospital, now described as at Manassas., but he has returned in November and December of 1861. The period January and February 1862 contains three notations: he is again absent sick; he is absent without leave; and he re-enlists, receiving a $50 bounty. April through June 1862 finds him absent, wounded. The next recorded event is in September 1863, when he is marked "Present." He is absent "detailed" November and December 1863. There is no record for the first two months of 1864. In April 1864 he is detailed to "Headquarters, 19th Virginia Infantry:" May and June detailed to hospital duty, and during July and August "detailed to the Secretary of War." There his service record ends.

_vidence in the case to be certified to the Auditor
of Public Accounts.

To the Hon. Tho. P. Fitzpatrick Judge of the County
Court of Nelson County:
                    Your petitioner Willis C.
Wills respectfully represents that he is a citizen
of Virginia, and during the late war between
the United States & the Confederate States he was
a citizen of Virginia, and was engaged in military
service in the Confederate States army, being
a member of Company G. 19th Va. Regiment,
and that while so engaged he was wounded
in the left arm between the shoulder and
the elbow and that he is as much and as
permanently disabled by reason of said wound
as if he had actually lost a limb, and that
said wound was received at the battle of
Williamsburg on the 5th day of May 1862. That
he is dependent on his physical labor for means
of subsistence. That he has not within five
years received an artificial arm or commutation money from this state, but that he
did receive commutation money in 1876 or 77.
                    Willis C. Wills.
Lovingston, Nelson Co: Va.
Sworn to before me in open court this

In his application for a pension, he stated, "...he was wounded in the left arm between the shoulder and the elbow and that he is as much permanently disabled by reason of said wound as if he had actually lost a limb." The wound occurred at the Battle of Winchester, May 5, 1862. His assertion is verified by a sworn statement from Drs. W. M. Eubank, A. B. Fitzpatrick, and Wm. S. Dillard, who described "a wound in the middle of the left humerus, causing a permanent contracture of the left hand." In the attached document, Willis presented his case to Hon. Ths. P. Fitzpatrick, Judge of the County Clerk of Nelson County. In this application Willis states that he is "dependent upon physical labor." There is no record of why he did not return to his vocation of schoolmaster. He was awarded a pension of $15 per year.

Armistead W. Wills enlisted in Company H, 44th Virginia Infantry, signing with an "X," at Crab Bottom, Highland County. (The village's name was changed to Blue Grass, ZIP code 24413, in 1950.) Wills was in the hospital at Richmond in June 1862, for reasons not recorded. He was wounded at Culp's Hill, July 2, 1863, during the Battle of Gettysburg, and arrived at Richmond's Chimborazo Hospital on July 20, 1863. He was well enough to be with his regiment at Spotsylvania when he was captured May 12, 1864. After a stay at Point Lookout, he was paroled five months later at Elmira, New York, site of a large prisoner of war camp. In his somewhat hard to read pension application he stated the wound (or wounds) had caused "his foot being drawn up by contraction of the sinews." Dr. James W. (illegible) certified that he found "the muscles of the (illegible) side of left thigh much injured by an apparent gunshot wound, and the use of the right foot greatly impaired by another wound inside of the right knee, constituting together so great a degree of bodily injury and to render him ... incapable of useful manual labor."

Application for Aid to Citizens of Virginia Wounded and Maimed during the late War.

Virginia:

In the Hustings Court of the City of Petersburg County, May 7th 1884.

Upon the application of Armistead W. Wills for aid under an act of the General Assembly approved February 25, 1884, entitled "An act to give aid to the citizens of Virginia wounded and maimed during the late war, while serving as Soldiers or Marines."

The Court having carefully considered the written application of the said Armistead W. Mills verified by his oath, and the evidence adduced in support of said application, is of opinion that the said Armistead W. Mills is entitled to aid under said act, and directs the said application and all the evidence in the case to be certified to the Auditor of Public Accounts.

[Here insert the application and evidence.]

Your affiant states that he was a private in Captain T. N. Coleman's Company 44th Va Regiment Johnson's Division Ewell's Corps in the late War, that he was wounded at Gettysburg on the 2nd day of July 1863 and is now using his ankle to walk on, the foot being drawn to one side by contraction of the sinews caused by the said wound. That he has not received any commutation money or bounty or pension from the State of Virginia or from any other state or from the United States of America or any artificial limb from any or either of them.
Given under my hand this 5th day of May 1884

Witness D H Lane — Armistead W. Mills (his mark)

Sworn to before me May 5 1884
D H Thompson JP City Petersburg

Petersburg May 5th 1884. This is to certify that I have carefully examined the condition of Mr. Armistead W. Mills formerly of Company H 44th Virginia Infantry and find the muscle of the outer side of left thigh much injured by an apparent gunshot wound, and the use of the right foot greatly impaired by another wound inside of right knee constituting together so great a degree of bodily injury as has rendered him heretofore and will render him hereafter incapable of useful manual labor

James W. Claiborne MD

Sworn to before me this 6 May 1884 — Jno. L. Armistead Clk Hust. Ct. Pbg

Full name of applicant Armistead W. Mills

Residence Petersburg Va

Post office address 9 Franklin St Petersburg Va

A copy—Teste: John L. Armistead Clerk.

William H. Abbott enlisted in Company A, 53rd Va. Infantry September 18, 1861 at Deep Creek. He was absent sick July - August 1862 and January - February 1863. He was back in the hospital again March and April 1863, this time at Charlottesville, with a diagnosis of "Debilitas." He was well enough to join his regiment at Gettysburg, where he was wounded in the right hip.

Two months later he rejoined his regiment, only to be absent sick again in August 1864, from a gunshot wound in the left shoulder suffered at Danville in June 1864. There his military record ends. He applied for a pension for the first time in March 1882. A medical certificate cites a Minié ball wound which injured his right hip and thigh "which cut the muscles of the thigh connecting with the hip." He was rated partially disabled for his usual work as a farmer. Abbott's application was apparently rejected. He reapplied in March 1884. An affidavit signed by Drs. H. B. Melvin, L. Faulkner, and I. Grammer noted "a gunshot wound of the right hip, in front of and to the inner part of the Great Trochanter, injuring to a very great extent the Vastus Externus at this point of its origin. This is the largest of the extensor muscles of the thigh and used to extend and raise the leg." Abbott received no pension. Perhaps his personal wealth exceeded the then limit, but no reason appears in the records.

Francis Willis, of Company H, 50th Va. Infantry, is one of those soldiers whose case defies clarification. Fragments of record say he had two fingers shot off at Kellys Lane and that his hand was crippled from a horse's kick at Suffolk. In May 1882 he received a commutation check of $60, the largest possible pension amount, yet he re-applied in 1884. The one document from his latter application, a physician's affidavit, is very hard to read.

The case of Robert J. Adams of Company H, 22nd Va. Inf. Battalion (not Regiment) was somewhat confused, since Rodgers' roster listed him as S. M. Adams. The latter Adams was his widow Sarah, nee Shepherd, who had three children at home. (John was born in 1858; Robert was born in 1863; we could not identify a third child.) Robert, a native of Fluvanna County, enlisted January 31, 1863 at Camp Lee. He was killed five months later in the first days' fighting at Gettysburg. Sarah filed a widow's claim on October 25, 1864, however the slips of paper in the Library of Virginia's files are dated in 1888. On April 20 of that year Judge A. E. King certified that he had carefully reviewed the evidence in her case and approved her application for a yearly payment of thirty dollars.

[OFFICIAL FORM.]

Application of a Widow of a Deceased Soldier, Sailor or Marine for a Pension.

I, _S. M. Adams_, residing at _Near Chincoteague_ in the _County_ of _Fluvanna_ In State of Virginia, do hereby apply for aid under an act of the General Assembly entitled "An act to give aid to soldiers, sailors, or marines of Virginia, maimed or disabled in the war between the States, and to the widows of Virginia soldiers, sailors and marines who lost their lives in said war in the military service." And I do swear that I am the widow of _Robert J. Adams_ who was a member of _Co. K 22 9th Battalion, Wise's Brigade_ and who, while in the discharge of his duty in military service during the late war between the States, lost his life. And I do further swear that I am not receiving aid from or a pension from any State or from the United States, and that I do not hold any national, State or county office which pays me in fees or salary over three hundred dollars; that my income from no source amounts to three hundred dollars; and that I do not own in my own right property of the assessed value of one thousand dollars; and that I am now entitled to receive annually the sum of thirty dollars under the terms of the aforesaid act of the General Assembly.

And I do further swear that the following answers are true:

1st. What was the name of the applicant's deceased husband? Ans. _Scott J. Adams_

2d. When and where, as nearly as can be ascertained, did the applicant's husband die, and from what cause? Ans. _At Gettysburg in the first days fight in July 1863_

3d. When and where were the applicant and here deceased husband married? Ans. _In Fluvanna Co. Va._

4th. Has the applicant ever married again? Ans. _No_

S. M. Adams

I, _A. E. King_, Judge of the _County_ Court for the _County_ of _Fluvanna_ do certify that _Mrs. S. M. Adams_, whose name is signed to the foregoing application, personally appeared before me in open court, and, having the said application fully read and explained to her, as well as the statements and answers therein made, she the said _Mrs. S. M. Adams_ made oath before me that said statements and answers are true.

Given under my hand this _23rd_ day of _April_, 18 88

A. E. King

VIRGINIA:

County of *Bedford*, TO-WIT:

I, *Micajah Davis*, Judge of the *County* Court for the *County* of *Bedford*, do certify that I have carefully enquired and examined into, and am fully satisfied from the evidence adduced before me that each and all of the facts set forth in the within application are true; that the applicant is the identical person named in the application; that the application is for these reasons approved, and is therefore certified that

Henry Wills

is entitled to receive annually from the State of Virginia the sum of *Fifteen* dollars

Given under my hand this *2nd* day of *May* 188*9*

Henry Wills, age 30, was mustered into Company A (Walker Guards), 58th Va. Infantry, September 30, 1861, at Staunton. He was listed as "Present" November 1861 through September 1864, at which time he was listed as "Killed in Action at Winchester." This was inaccurate. He had been captured at Winchester after being wounded. The extant Union record tells us: "Henry Wills, Sgt. Co. A, 58 Reg't VA, wounded at Winchester Sept. 19, 1864, ball entered right side of back and escaped in (illegible), Slt. Treatment Simple dressings." He was sent first to U.S.A. Gen'l Hosp, West's Buildings, Baltimore, Md. From thence to Point Lookout. He was exchanged in December 1864 and given a 30-day sick furlough in January 1865. On May 2, 1888 he was awarded a yearly payment of $15, for partial disability. His Virginia pension file is lacking medical information.

The service records of William Adams have proved some-what elusive. Rodgers lists him as Co. A, 42nd Virginia Battalion of Cavalry. Lee Wallace's reference tells us "42nd Bn.Va. Cav. See 24th Regt. Va. Cav." Adams' CMSR shows him enlisting in March 1862 at Henry Courthouse, into Co. H, 24th Va. Cavalry, also listed as 42nd Battalion Va. Cavalry. He was absent in Castle Thunder prison from November 1863 through February 1864, fol-lowing a general court-martial. He is listed as absent without leave in March 1864, but in that same month he is also described as being in a smallpox hospital in Richmond and being trans-ferred to the 25th Va. Infantry. In his CMSR there is no mention of a horse-related injury. In an 1886 pension application he states that "I belonged to Capt. I. R. Robertson's Co. A Col. Balls and Gen Garies [probably Gen. Martin W. Gary] brigade of cav-alry and whilst double quickening to go to engage the enemy my horse fell and caught my leg under him and in that condition was ridden over by other troops and crippled in my leg back and breast and the disability is so great that I have been unable to perform my duties on my farm." (He signed with an "X.") A com-rade George L. Allen swore under oath that he dismounted, saved Adams from further harm, and remembered that Adams was able to do only light duty after his injury. Jno. Bishop, M.D. wrote "...from his general appearance he is in a debilitated con-dition and unable to do as much work." The Auditor rejected the claim. "The physician's certificate is wholly insufficient. Must state character of wound and extent of wound." Papers filed in 1888 were approved and Adams received a pension of $15 per year, usually reflecting a conclusion of partial disability.

Virginia:

IN THE _County_ COURT OF _Patrick_ COUNTY.

March Term 1886.

Upon the application of _Wm Adams_ for aid under an act of the General Assembly, approved February 25, 1884, entitled "An act to give aid to the citizens of Virginia wounded and maimed during the late war, while serving as Soldiers or Marines."

The Court having carefully considered the written application of the said _Wm Adams_ verified by his oath, and the evidence adduced in support of said application, is of opinion that the said _Adams_ is entitled to aid under said act, and directs the said application and all the evidence in the case to be certified to the Auditor of Public Accounts.

[Here insert the application and evidence.]

I William Adams of Patrick Co. Va on oath declare that I was a Confederate soldier and belonged to Capt J. R. Robinson Co. A Col Balls and Gen. Carters brigade of Cavalry and whilst double quickening to go to engage the enemy my horse fell and caught my leg under him and in that condition was ridden over by the other troops and crippled in my leg back and breast and the disability is so great that I have been unable to discharge my duties on my farm the disability is permanent I have never recieved any commutation in way of money eye arm or leg from the state of Va or the United States I was a Virginian at the time I was so wounded and remain a Virginian

Wm Adams + his mark

I hereby on oath declare that I belonged to the same Co. with Wm Adams and saw his horse fall and upon him and would probably have killed him had I not have gotten down and rendered him my services – he was so badly hurt that he never did much service after that but light duty

George L. Allen

Sworn to before me this 23 March 1886 Jo Bishop J.P.

I have examined Wm Adams and from his general appearance he is in a debilitated condition and unable to do much work. Jno. L. Bishop M.D.

Sworn to by Dr. Jno. L. Bishop before me this 23 March 1886

Jo Bishop J.P.

Full name of applicant, _William Adams_
Residence, _Patrick Co. Va_
Post Office address,

L. A. P. d.c.

Albert J. Acree (some records mistakenly have him as Albon J. Acree) served in Capt. Kirkpatrick's Company, Amherst Artillery, and died at Lynchburg July 10, 1862. Some records say killed in action. His widow's application says he died of typhoid fever. He was survived by Ann Elizabeth "Nannie" Acree, nee Cheatwood, and at least three children, Thomas (b. 1855), Edward (b. 1857), and Leighton (b. 1859). On July 17, 1888, Judge C. P. Latham of the City of Lynchburg signed a certification that she qualified for a yearly pension of thirty dollars.

[OFFICIAL FORM.]

Application of a Widow of a Deceased Soldier, Sailor or Marine for a Pension.

I, *Nannie E. Acree*, residing at *Lynchburg*, in the County of *Campbell*, in State of Virginia, do hereby apply for aid under an act of the General Assembly entitled "An act to give aid to soldiers, sailors, or marines of Virginia, maimed or disabled in the war between the States, and to the widows of Virginia soldiers, sailors and marines who lost their lives in said war in the military service." And I do swear that I am the widow of *Albon J. Acree* who was a member of *the Amherst Artillery (Confederate States army) commanded by Capt. T. J. Kirkpatrick* and who, while in the discharge of his duty in military service during the late war between the States, lost his life. And I do further swear that I am not receiving aid from or a pension from any State or from the United States, and that I do not hold any national, State or county office which pays me in fees or salary over three hundred dollars; that my income from no source amounts to three hundred dollars; and that I do not own in my own right property of the assessed value of one thousand dollars; and that I am now entitled to receive annually the sum of thirty dollars under the terms of the aforesaid act of the General Assembly.

And I do farther swear that the following answers are true:

1st. What was the name of the applicant's deceased husband? Ans. *Albon J. Acree*

2d. When and where, as nearly as can be ascertained, did the applicant's husband die, and from what cause? Ans. *July 10th 1862, at Lynchburg Va. from typhoid fever contracted in service in the army*

3d. When and where were the applicant and her deceased husband married? Ans. *Bedford Co Va March 15th 1852*

4th. Has the applicant ever married again? Ans. *No*

Nannie E. Acree

I, *C. P. Latham*, Judge of the *Corporation* Court for the *City* of *Lynchburg* do certify that *Nannie E. Acree*, whose name is signed to the foregoing application, personally appeared before me in open court, and, having the said application fully read and explained to her, as well as the statements and answers therein made, she the said *Nannie E. Acree* made oath before me that said statements and answers are true.

Given under my hand this *10th* day of *July*, 18 88 *C. P. Latham*

Samuel F. Abrahams enlisted in Company D, 56th Va. Inf. July 8, 1861 at Staunton. He was wounded June 2, 1864 at Cold Harbor. "Wounded by Minié ball fracturing the surgical neck of the humerus, amputated at shoulder joint on the field, same day." He was then sent to Wayside Hospital in Richmond, thence to Chimborazo Hospital, then home to Hardwicksville on a sixty-day furlough. In August 1864 a medical board approved his retirement because he was "unfit for the duties of a soldier in field service because of loss of right arm" In 1886 he wrote a letter stating that he had been given an artificial arm, that it was useless, and that he had tried to return it and that some government office had refused to accept the return. He asked for "commutation," and in 1888 was awarded $30 a year pension.

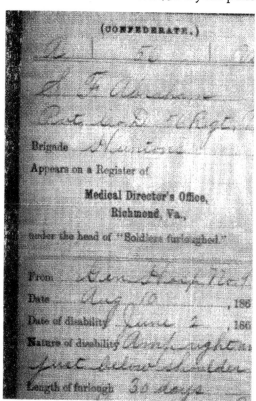

John E. Abernathy, who was five feet and eight inches tall, enlisted July 10, 1861 in Company E, 56th Va. Inf. at Sturgeonsville. In February 1862 he was captured at Fort Donelson. After a stay as a POW at Camp Morton he was exchanged at Vicksburg. In November 1862 he was four days in CSA General Hospital No. 3 in Richmond. In July 1863 he was wounded at Gettysburg but was well enough to make his way to Greencastle, Pa. before he was captured on July 7, 1863. He was admitted July 12, 1863 to Satterlee USA General Hospital at West Philadelphia, with a note, "prisoner of war, gunshot wound." He seems to have been paroled, because he was captured for the third time, April 6, 1865, at Farmville. He ended the war at Point Lookout prison camp. In 1888 he applied for a pension. "On July 3, 1863 I received a wound in my left groin by pieces of shell rendering left leg useless, in (the) charge at Gettysburg." He was awarded $15 per year. In 1902 he filled out "Application of Soldier, Sailor or Marine for Disability by Reason of Disease or the Infirmities of Age." The image is badly pixilated. There appear to be a doctor's certificate, sworn testimony by two comrades, and a recommendation by his local United Confederate Veterans camp. The final entry is from the Office of the Auditor of Public Accounts, stating that his application cannot be processed until it is complete. The "groin" wound was probably thigh rather than genital, since he had two sons. John A. Abernathy was born in 1873, followed by Fenton T. Abernathy in 1875. The solder is buried beneath a government-issued headstone, in the Abernathy Cemetery, Alberta, Brunswick County.

James J. Abbott, at age 32, enlisted in Company A, 58th Va. Infantry, on September 30, 1861 at Staunton. A month later he was admitted to Stribling Springs Hospital, where he remained until February of the following year. He did one month of duty in March 1862, but in April he was sent home on a sick furlough which lasted until November 1862, at which time he was admitted to Liberty Hospital. There he stayed for nine months, going AWOL in July 1863. He returned to Liberty Hospital and stayed there until his death August 31, 1863. Abbott's entry in Rodgers' 1888 roster states, "Killed in action. 1864 at home. Died of consumption. Abbott Sally S. 1888 application approved $30." Several attempts to find the pension records for both Sally and James at the Library of Virginia found nothing. The 1860 census has James and Sally, together with their son Jno. Abbott. James is not listed on Findagrave.com. The discrepancies in the records and his performance of almost no useful duty are unusual.

Joshua (J. T.) Adams was in Company G, 8th Va. Inf. in May 1862 when he was in Chimborazo Hospital with "Intermitt," which usually meant malaria. June 10, 1862 he died of scarlatina at Lynchburg General Hospital No. 2. Other records in the same file show him transferring to (or enlisting in) Company G, 21st Va. Cav. at Floyd Courthouse. At Front Royal, November 1864, he is recorded as having received a gunshot wound to the right knee and a saber wound which fractured the left parietal bone. He was taken prisoner and treated in the hospital at Point Lookout. In June 1865 he was still in a Union hospital although exchanged in February 1865. In his 1888 pension application he described "a sabre cut on the head which passed thru the skull making a cut of near four inches in length from the effects of said wound he is more or less disabled and at times he is unable to perform manual labor and is unable to lay on his left side while in bed." He was awarded $15 per year. (Reconciling his 1862 death with his later service has puzzled the author.)

Adams' saber wound was a very unusual event in the vast panorama of the Civil War. Almost every painting of cavalry action shows men hacking at each other with their sabers, a dramatic scene indeed. However, of the 358,529 Union soldiers who died in the war, only 26 were killed by saber wounds, or roughly 0.0007 percent. The man who wrote the script for Mel Gibson's *Braveheart* told a reporter, "If you have the history and you have the legend, always go with the legend."

These sample cases illustrate both the riches to be found in these hallowed records and the limitations and frustrations in attempting a complete understanding of the stories of the soldiers and their wounds and diseases. They are also a contrast with the detailed records of today. Joshua Adams records, if made today, would probably include a skull x-ray, an MRI, an electroencephalogram, and some neuropsychological testing.

CHAPTER 5

DOUBLE DIPPERS?

In the author's *Galvanized Virginians in the Indian Wars*, page 197, there is listed six men who seemed to be "double dippers," men who collected pensions from both North and South, or who had collected Confederate pensions or veteran's home care even though they had also served in the Union Army. The ability to research such issues has been greatly enhanced by the Library of Virginia's digitized records available online. They include both "Confederate Disability Applications and Receipts," and "Confederate Pension Rolls, Veterans and Widows." While the digitized records are, for the most part, easily readable, in some records a combination of pixilation and dreadful handwriting renders them unusable.

Using a combination of the enlistment and service records of Virginia Confederate soldiers and the enlistment and service records of the same men in the United States Volunteers (both available of Fold3.com), followed by a search of the Confederate pension records described above, it is possible, with a fair degree of certainty, to discern whether any of these men were indeed double dippers.

(The abbreviation "CMSR" indicates Compiled Military Service Record. The origins, reproductions, and availability of these records, both North and South, are fully analyzed in *Galvanized Virginians*, pages 198-200.)

Isaac C. Jenkins enlisted in Co. L, 10th Virginia Infantry in August 1861 at "Camp Johnson." He was AWOL from October 1861 to January 1862, and deserted in April 1862. His return date is not recorded. He was wounded at Chancellorsville May 2, 1863, sent to hospital, and went AWOL in August 1863. Again, a return date is not noted. He was captured in August 1864 at Bermuda Hundred (CMSR). He was held prisoner at Point Lookout, where two months later, he was mustered into Co. E, 4th US Volunteers. He was soon in jail in Norfolk, Virginia, from whence he escaped and never returned (CMSR). In April 1886, at the age of forty-three, he applied for a Virginia pension based on disability caused by "...a Minié ball wound in the right temple." He further claimed "... can do no work which requires standing, cannot perform more than one-third of the manual labor that he did before the war ... disability equal to the loss of a limb." He signed with an "X." In an affidavit sworn before the Clerk of the Page County, Jenkins stated that after his wound he was "so seriously and permanently disabled as to be afterwards incapacitated for said service until the close of the said war." He also swore that he had "never received any kind of commutation, money, or pension from this or any other states, or from the United states ... and makes oath that the statements ... are correct and true." A doctor, whose signature is illegible, swore that Jenkins was disabled, and an equally illegible comrade swore that he personally knew of Jenkins' wound.

In June 1887, Jenkins' attorney "received of Auditor of Public Accounts check No. 9256 of Planters National Bank for $60 [roughly $1800 in 2016 money]; the same being payment in full of the commutation money allowed me by the Act of the General Assembly of Virginia of 1885-1886, making an appropriation to maimed and disabled solders." (Pension records). Jenkins in his sworn statements omitted his Confederate service at Bermuda Hundred, his time as a prisoner at Point Lookout, and his service, however brief, as a soldier in the United States Volunteers. He was a documented double dipper. His remains lie in the Western State Hospital Cemetery at Staunton.

George W. Taylor was a very popular name. In the US Volunteers there were three such: Co. 5th USV; Co. F, 1st USV; and Co. G, 2nd USV. The man in the 1st USV seems most likely, and the Virginia records for a possible candidate suggest three possible antecedents for Federal service.

First: George W. Taylor enlisted in Co. A, 23rd Va. Inf. at Staunton Courthouse, signing with an "X." He was AWOL in July 1862 but present that September. He was wounded May 2, 1863, a gunshot fracturing his right femur. After a long stay at

Chimborazo Hospital he was returned to duty January 1865, at which time a medical board, noting that one leg was shorter than the other, declared him "not fit for duty in any branch." (CMSR) In November 1887 he applied for a Virginia pension under the act of that year, citing the wound described earlier. (Pension records) He is clearly not a veteran of the US Volunteers.

Second: George W. Taylor of Co. B, 56th Va. Inf. was captured, wounded, at Greencastle, Pa.; he was treated at Chester, Pa. with a flaxseed poultice, before he was transferred to Hammond Hospital at Point Lookout. He was paroled March 1864 and three months later was at Chimborazo Hospital (Richmond, Va.) for treatment of syphilis. In 1886, he applied for a Virginia pension, stating that he was "wounded in the charge at Gettysburg, July 3, 1863. The ball is still in my thigh." (His regiment was in the midst of the charge—Garnett's Brigade, Pickett's Division.)

Third: George W. Taylor enlisted in May 1861 in Co. A, 55th Va. Inf., at Lowry's Point, a cape in Essex County. He was absent sick in June 1862 but back on duty by that December. He was captured at Falling Waters, Pa. in mid-July 1863 and sent to Point Lookout via Old Capitol Prison. On February 25, 1864 he enlisted in Co. F, 1st US Volunteers. One record states that he died of disease December 22, 1864 while another says he deserted the US Volunteers at Elizabeth City. There are at least four George W. Taylors who applied for Virginia pensions. None of these seem to be from the 55th Va. Inf. Findagrave.com lists sixty-eight George W. Taylors buried in Virginia. The status of all these men seems to be a hopeless tangle, with no clear evidence of double dipping.

James R. Patton enlisted in Company A, 63rd Va. Inf. in March 1862 at Abington. He deserted four months later, not returning until January 1864. There is no record of a court-martial. He was captured May 20, 1864 near Calhoun, Ga., and held a prisoner at Rock Island. He enlisted as a corporal in Company K, 2nd US Volunteers October 13, 1864, where he is listed as "Patton" and "Patten." He was honorably discharged November 18, 1865. In April 1883 he applied for a Union disability pension, which he apparently received. He died January 6, 1916 and is buried in Speedwell Methodist Cemetery, Wythe County, Va. Curiously his widow's application is dated February 1914.

A James R. Patton applied for a Virginia pension in 1900, stating "I am broken down in my back and hips." Several doctors certified him as "various diseases...lumbago...general infirmity... and breakdown of whole system." However, a closer inspection of the blurred record shows him to have been a member of the 45th Va. Inf., who died in 1908. Nor should he be confused with James Houston Patton of the 1st Va. Inf., an engineer and later physician, whose 1900 application was based on locomotor ataxia, a form of tertiary syphilis. It would appear that our James R. Patton of the 63rd Va. Inf. made only one pension application and that was for his Union service. No double dipper, he.

Gordon H. Lane enlisted in Company C, 54th Va. Inf. September 10, 1861 at Christiansburg, signing with an "X." He was captured near Marietta, Ga. July 3, 1864, and was shipped to

Camp Douglas prison via Louisville. (Confederate CMSR) While a prisoner at Camp Douglas he enlisted in Company C, 6th US Volunteers and served in Nebraska Territory. He was mustered out at Fort Kearney in October 1866 and in 1907 applied for a Union pension (Pension records). In 1910 while living at Vicar/Vicker, Montgomery County, he applied for a Virginia pension. The application clearly lists his old regiment as 54th Va. Inf. The application was based on "disability by reason of rheumatism and age." In answer to the question "When and why did you leave the service?" he replied "I was captured 1863 or 1864 and kept a prisoner 16 months." He made no mention of his Union service or Union pension. Former comrades H. Harman and H. F. Laudbaugh (their names are blurred) swore that they were "satisfied at the justice of his claims." Lane received his first Virginia check May 11, 1910. (Virginia state records).

He died February 16, 1914 and is buried in Den Hill Cemetery, Montgomery County. His tombstone, weathered and lichen-encrusted, sits high on a grassy slope of apparently abandoned monuments. In 1917, his widow applied for a Union pension; she lived until 1935. It appears that Gordon Lane was a documented double dipper.

Jacob Heater, at the age of eighteen, enlisted in Company D, 31st Virginia Infantry. A few weeks later he was captured at Red House, Va. and exchanged in August 1861. He was captured again, this time at Harris Farm, Va., in May 1864, and sent to Point Lookout. There he enlisted in Company I, 1st US Volunteers. After a few months of service, he deserted the Union army at Bloomington Ferry, Mn. Virginia benefits were denied to men who had served in the Union army, but by the 1920s Heater was living in the Confederate Veterans Home in Richmond, Va. There he earned a little extra money by selling cards of himself, each card also carrying text of sentimental doggerel. He died May 11, 1930 at the home. He is not in the Hollywood Cemetery roster. Indeed, a double dipper.

CHAPTER 6
FRAUD, GLORIOUS FRAUD

In 1951, a Civil War commemoration was held in Norfolk, Virginia. Among those honored were three of the oldest living Confederates. Left to right: John Salling, William Townsend, and William Bush. Earlier in the day they had appeared in their custom-made gray uniforms. *Photo: Virginian-Pilot.*

Here we see one of those treasured moments in American history—brave men now ancient, gathered together for one last time, each of them over a century old, messengers sent to us from the past, living monuments to The Cause for which they fought so bravely. Yet there quivers in the air a tiny note of doubt. Deeper delving into their courageous stories brings us to two almost forgotten names: Baron Munchausen and Lieut. J. W. Boyer.

Once there was a real Munchausen: Baron Hieronymus Karl Friedrich, Freiherr von Münchausen. Based on this actual man, German writer Rudolph Erich Raspe created a fictional baron, whose extraordinary exploits, fabricated adventures, and wildly inconsistent tall tales first made it into print in 1785 as *Baron von Munchausen's Narrative of his Marvelous Travels and Campaigns in Russia*. Two centuries later his legacy lives on as Munchausen's Syndrome, an often-debated psychiatric condition.

This condition is one in which the "patient" is feigning disease or a history of suffering in order to get attention, special care, or sympathy. Within the casual sub-dialect of medical workers it has such colorful names as "hospital addiction syndrome," "thick chart syndrome," "hospital hopper syndrome," and "Gomer," an acronym for Get Out of My Emergency Room. Many Munchausen travelers are quite well-informed about what complaints will elicit medical concern and care. Whether this condition is out and out conscious fraud, or a mental pattern that the patient has come to actually believe, is not easily answered.

Was J. W. Boyer, a former lieutenant in the 184th Pennsylvania Infantry, an example of Munchausen's Syndrome? A truck traveling the highway outside of Reno on a hot July day in 1951 stopped to give a ride to an old man, struggling with a 30-pound bag. The trucker dropped him off at the Red Cross shelter, where he spent the night, regaling the manager with the story of his search for his great-great-grandson. The next morning, Boyer hoisted his bag and started down Virginia Street, where he collapsed on the sidewalk. Soon he was in Washoe General Hospital, being treated for a probable heart attack. After a few hours in an oxygen tent, he perked up and told the staff that he was 104 years old and charmed them with his memories of the Civil War. Apparently in deference to his long-ago loyal service, he was soon in a private room with his own private nurse. His story quickly prompted a visit from the local newspaper. They published a photo of him enjoying a big steak dinner. The Washoe County Medical Society paid his hospital bill. The ladies' auxiliary of the GAR sent him flowers. Concerned about this old soldier, the hospital contacted the Veteran's Administration and the War Department. They found no record of such a veteran. When his doctor brought him this news, Boyer had another heart attack and was quickly back in an oxygen tent. When he felt better, he told the hospital staff that he had been "confused," that his Civil War service had actually been in Indiana, but the Indiana GAR had no record of him. Boyer objected and produced some yellow papers from his bag, but none of them had his name on them. About this time the Veteran's Administration solved the puzzle. Lieut. Boyer was, in actual fact, Walter Engle Urwiler, age sixty-nine, who for years had been traveling the country, having "heart attacks," on the public streets and earning himself a comfortable hospital bed.

Further research showed that at various hospitals he had claimed be a veteran of every American war from 1861 to 1945. He had also told tall tales about his careers as a fur trapper, deep-sea diver, naval officer, miner, and sheriff. When confronted with this history, he stomped out of the Reno hospital and was soon having a "heart attack" on the streets of Susanville, California. There, a very perceptive physician, Arthur Bachelor, walked into the room occupied by the old fraud and told him no more comfy bed and no more free meals. It was time to go. Urwiler leaped out of bed, grabbed his sack, and headed north where, a few days later, he had yet another heart attack, this one in Tacoma, Washington. At the county hospital he was now Robert Larson, still a Civil War veteran. Another wise doctor discovered the man's ability to manipulate his heart rate and arranged for a different bed, this one in jail. He told a series of wild stories to Judge Frank Hale, who gave Boyer/Urwiler/Larson sixty days in jail for vagrancy. Within a week after his release he had yet another heart attack, this one in San Antonio, Texas. How long his saga continued is lost in the clichéd "mists of time."

Which brings us to John Salling, of the village of Slant, Virginia, where he has not one but two monuments. The first was one issued and paid for by the Federal government as a courtesy to long-dead Confederates. The second one is a six-foot tall granite slab paid for and erected by the Virginia Division of the United Daughters of the Confederacy in 1961.

The origin of the smaller stone is shown in the "Application for Headstone or Marker," dated March 23, 1959, filed by Mrs. Euna McCamy, daughter of the veteran, address Route 1, Fort Blackmore, Virginia. She gave his Confederate service as "25th Virginia, Co. D," and date of birth as "May 5, 1846." The order was placed with the Georgia Marble Co. of Tate, Georgia, with instructions that the stone be delivered by freight at Gate City, with installation in "Salling Cemetery, Slant, Virginia." The Compiled Military Service Records of the 25th Virginia Infantry, held in the National Archives, contain no Salling.

Slant is a cluster of homes, some abandoned, scattered along State Highway 65 in Scott County. It has no ZIP code. The chief attractions are the monuments shown above and a small Methodist church. But what is the history of Salling himself?

His disputed military service was an issue in the many interviews with reporters and well-wishers, especially his absence from the regimental records. Salling said it was because he had been assigned to be a "peter boy," rather than a musket-toting soldier. "Peter" was saltpeter, a naturally occurring form of potassium nitrate. Every boy who ever contemplated mischief knows that gunpowder is made from charcoal, sulfur, and potassium nitrate. The peter boys crawled into caves in the

Virginia hills, dug the saltpeter, stuffed it in bags, and hauled the sacks out to the cave's mouth—nasty, backbreaking work. The peter boys were indeed of great benefit to the Confederate munitions industry, but there are no records showing Salling as one of them.

His career as a professional veteran began in the depths of the Great Depression. For half a century after the Civil War he had been able to support himself, a wife, and many children up in the hills by cooking moonshine and by farming. But he was getting old, Prohibition was ending, with loss of the moonshine trade. It was time to try for a pension. In 1933 he applied for a Virginia State Confederate veteran's pension. The correspondence focused on the many discrepancies in his story. After almost a year, Salling dropped his attempts. He was never awarded a pension, but his claims of extreme age and his cheerful cornball humor was just what reporters needed to spice up a day. He was full of moonshiner stories and tales of pretty girls. Fame led to fame. Someone paid for an airplane ride, to attend the 1951 gathering in Norfolk. Two years later, he was flown to West Virginia to be honored by the Patriotic Sons of America. There he wore his new Confederate uniform, donated by the Women's Army Corps at Fort Myer, Virginia. The gray cloth was enlivened by a startling cluster of colorful medals. By now, it would seem unmannerly to doubt the bona fides of this charming ancient one. The Virginia General Assembly awarded him a soldier's bonus of $500 and an honorary military pension of $135 a month.

His reputed great age even earned him a personal commendation from Dwight D. Eisenhower, whose own military service is both better known and better documented,

'Gen.' John Salling Has 109th Birthday

Receives Greetings From Ike

Fort Blackmore Man Lone Virginia Confederate Veteran

FT. BLACKMORE, Va., May 15 — John B. Salling got a birthday cake today--much like any other birthday cake--but his had 109 candles on it.

The cake was only one of several surprises Virginia's only living Confederate veteran received today. The three-tier cake was given to him by a Bristol bakery.

The old gentleman also received a hat--one with a wide brim like he wanted--from a Bristol department store. He is rarely seen without a hat, something he says has helped keep his hair black. He also says he "never washed it," and claims that helped too.

The Big Stone Gap chapter of the United Daughters of the Confederacy gave him a Confederate flag.

But the high point of the day for Salling was receiving birthday greetings from President Eisenhower and Gov. Stanley. That made his day complete.

Salling, who lives near this tiny western Virginia mountain town with his daughter and son-in-law, Mr. and Mrs. Hughie McKamey, sat on the porch most of the day.

He wore a Confederate uniform given to him several years ago, bedecked with medals showing he has been through a number of tough campaigns—the reunions of confederate veterans he has attended.

He was in good spirits and had a joke or a story about the old days for all of his friends. All in all, it was a big occasion for the old Rebel and he appeared to enjoy immensely talking with his many visitors and well-wishers who trooped in all day.

BIRTHDAY FOR "GENERAL" JOHN—"General" JOHN B. SALLING of Ft. Blackmore, Virginia's only surviving Civil War veteran, poses for a birthday photograph. He was 109 Sunday. The General is one of the three Confederate Army survivors in the United States.

Russia Approves 'Summit' Meeting

Sometime in the 1950s Salling acquired the honorary title of general, a rank which appears on the monument set up by the United Daughters of the Confederacy. Salling had acquired a mythic, almost cult-like status. All the lost dreams of the Confederacy were projected upon this living, breathing symbol of all that was durable, free-spirited, indomitable, and unconquerable in the Old South. Perhaps it is even irrelevant that he was a fraud. And yet there is still some necessity that our nation's history be grounded in fact.

The final arbiter in the life of Salling is the United States Census. The findings of that nationwide data collection are in huge books, bound in red, housed in the National Archives. Many years ago they were microfilmed and the results are widely available, both online and in libraries. There is no known instance of fraud in either the collecting or recording of this data. Consider now these images, appearing on pages 197 and 198 in the section headed "Free Inhabitants in the County of Scott State of Virginia enumerated by me, on the 8th day of August 1860, John Hicks, Asst. Marshal." The last entry on page 197 is "Caroline M. Salling, age 84, female, Occupation weaver." She had real estate valued at $900 and personal property worth $800. This household is continued in the first two lines of page 198, where we see "Caroline M. Salling, age 30, spinster," and "John G. Salling, age 4." All three Sallings were born in Virginia. The two grave markers illustrated earlier give his birth year as 1846, a date preferred by his many modern-day supporters. A birth year of 1856 is almost certainly the correct one. Somewhere, somehow Salling added a decade to his age. (Further complexities in his case are that his mother never married and that the 1880 census lists him as "mulatto.")

William Lundy was another ancient Confederate veteran. The party was over, at least for William Lundy's reputation as a Confederate soldier. The unblinking eye of the census records does not confirm Lundy's self-told tales, as cheerful and as dramatic as they may have been. The relevant page is headed, "Free Inhabitants of the Southern Division in the County of Mobile State of Alabama enumerated by me on the 6th day of August 1860, J. J. Delabaugh, asst. marshal." Unlike many old records this one is on good white paper with black ink. There is no mistaking the family of James S. Lundy, a 25-year old shingle maker. With him is Jane Lundy, age 20, and their three children: Lofton age three, William age one, and Margaret age four months. The final member of the household is Abraham Lundy, age 77, a retired merchant.

Once again, heritage trumps history. His tombstone, paid for by the Federal taxpayers, is engraved, "WILLIAM AL-LEN LUNDY CO D 4 REGT ALA CAV CSA JAN 18 1848 SEPT 1 1957." Above the text is the Southern Cross of Honor, whose famous motto is *Deo vindice,* "God will vindicate us." We have no way of anticipating God's judgement in this matter, but the documented records support hardly any of the text above Lundy's final resting place.

The newspapers were kind to Lundy's memory. Investigative journalism is expensive and time-consuming. With a deadline every twenty-four hours, it is more practical just to print the information off the Associated Press wire service.

WM. A. LUNDY, 109, ONE OF LAST 3 VETS OF CIVIL WAR, DIES

Crestview, Fla., Sept. 2 [Monday] — (AP) — William A. Lundy, 109, one of the last three veterans of the Civil War, died in a hospital here last night. Lundy. born near Troy, Ala., Jan. 18, 1848, was taken to the hospital shortly after 8 p. m. He had resided with a son, Charlie, here for a year.

Lundy served with a Confederate home guard unit at Elba, Ala., during the closing days of the Civil war. He was 16 years old at the time.

Surviving Civil war veterans are Walter W. Williams, 114, of Franklin, Tex., and John B. Salling, 111, of Slant, Va. Both are Confederate veterans. The last Union veteran, Albert Woolson of Duluth, Minn., died last year. He was 109.

The Pelican State embraced William Daniel Townsend as one of their own. He often recounted his story of having joined the Confederate forces at age fifteen and was wounded, captured, and paroled at Vicksburg. After the war he settled in Olla, Louisiana, married four times, and lived in desperate poverty. In 1935, he applied for a Louisiana state pension. He claimed he had served under Capt. Gus Cobb. Pension officials could find no such Cobb. They suspected that he was trying to take credit for a W. Townsend, Company B, 27th Louisiana Infantry, whose age did not match this applicant. Not fazed by this rejection, he now claimed to have served with these comrades: John Orr, Jim Orr, Lum Knox, B. Russell, and Dave Seats. Pension officials could find no such men. Townsend now turned up ninety-two-year old Alf Fuller, who swore that he remembered a Willie Townsend from the 27th Louisiana. The Olla-dwelling Townsend finally got his $60 a month, but was dropped from the welfare rolls. He protested vigorously, seeking more money. His wife was unhappy, but for different reasons. She wrote to the welfare office, complaining that he spent his pension check away from the home, leaving no money for food. When this produced no results, she wrote to the Veterans Administration in Washington, DC. They, too, did not help her. In brief, Townsend received a pension, in spite of zero proof that he had ever served. In spite of all, as he passed on, the Federal government that he so despised honored him with a color guard, a brass band, taps, and a 21-rifle salute.

Bury 'Rebel' With Honors

SHREVEPORT, La. ⁄P⁄ — A military band played "Dixie" as the gray-clad body of Louisiana's last Confederate veteran was lowered into its grave.

William Townsend, 106-year-old survivor of the Battle of Vicksburg, was buried Tuesday with military honors—a National Guard color guard displaying the Confederate and American flags, an Air Force band and an honor guard of seven airmen.

Thus the state and federal government paid tribute to one of the last survivors of the War Between the States, one who said in 1938 that he had never sworn allegiance to the United States unless it was while he was wounded or under duress.

Townsend died Sunday night at his home at Olla, 100 miles southeast of here.

Taps and a 21-rifle salute sounded for Townsend, whose death left only four Confederate and two Union veterans.

Louis Nicholas Baker was a quiet and ancient resident of Guthrie, Oklahoma, who spent his days on the front steps of a business, slowly reading the paper with the aid of a large magnifying glass. When queried, he told tales of the frontier, such as his membership in the Anti-Horse Thief Association, formed in 1854. He came to public notice in 1956, when Albert Henry Woolson, the last known Union soldier, died. Baker suddenly proclaimed the he was now the oldest living Yankee soldier. This created a local buzz, but searching Federal records showed no evidence of his service, and his already dim memory grew dimmer with each passing week. He died January 19, 1957 and lies in Guthrie's Summit View Cemetery.

Quid est veritas? "(Pontius) Pilate saith unto him, 'What is truth'?" John 18:38. This might well be applied to self-created veteran William J. Bush, a shining example of "All hat and no cattle." In the 1940s he began to create himself as General Bush. He had a brief encounter with the movie industry, resulting in a $300 custom-made Confederate uniform, to which he added a red sash, usually the mark of an artillery officer. He was ever the flamboyant, self-promoting poseur. When his long-suffering wife graduated from college, William pushed himself to the front, boasting that he was getting younger every day, and that he planned to live to age 140. At the 1951 Norfolk conclave, he popped out of the car. made his way through a bevy of white-haired beauties, and in the hotel lobby shouted for whiskey, cigars, and women. As to his military service for his home state of Georgia, there was scant evidence. Although he had told reporters that he had been Robert E. Lee's body guard, had witnessed the surrender at Appomattox, and had fought bravely at Gettysburg, the Georgia state archives could find only a vaguely possible three months in the militia and the recorded times and dates totally excluded any possibility of his Appomattox and Gettysburg tales. In 1937, the state awarded him a pension, based on political pressure by his state senator. Bush happily collected his money until 1952, when he was carried off to the Valhalla of Ersatz Warriors. The Peach State mourned his passing by lowering flags to half-mast.

In 680 A.D., at the site of Karbala in present day Iraq, the Shia forces were crushed by the Sunnis in a bloody defeat. This event remains a bitter memory, kept vivid by annual commemorations. Thirteen hundred years have not erased this stain on their honor. At the Battle of Kosovo in 1389, the Christian Serbs were crushed by the Moslem Ottomans. Six centuries later the Serbs still recall that humiliating defeat and to this present day it plays a part in Balkan politics. Loss of honor, loss of "face," is a condition that rankles in the human soul.

And the defeated South was and is no exception. A century and a half later it seems like only yesterday when the soldiers of the Confederacy trudged home to overgrown farms, burned cities, and twisted railroad iron. And the ashes of defeat in their mouths. It was for the repair of their own souls that Southern men and women gave birth to the Lost Cause, with its hagiography of Confederate generals, its vague sense of having been cheated, and the presence of four million freed slaves a constant reminder of an enormous economic loss. And it was inevitable that ancient veterans, documented or not, were symbols of an unvanquished spirit and as vehicles for restored honor and lost chivalry. The more ancient the better, each centenarian becoming living proof that the South was somehow undying and morally victorious.

No better example of Southern Immortality Through Honored Veterans can be found than that of Walter Williams. He told many interviewers that he had been enlisted in the 5th Texas Infantry, part of Hood's Brigade. He recalled eleven months as a forager ("I stole food.") as Hood's forces passed through Mississippi. When the war was over he moved to an isolated farm outside Franklin, Texas, where he farmed, drove cattle on the Chisholm Trail, married twice, and had many children. He made little fuss about either himself or his role in the war. In 1932, near the depth of the Great Depression, he tried for a Texas veteran's pension, as a hedge against the dreadful poverty of the decade. The application was granted on the word of a local judge and two neighbors, who swore Williams was of good character and that they believed Williams was telling the truth when he claimed service in the 5th Texas Infantry. (The CMSRs available on Fold3.com do not show a Walter Williams.) He remained a man little known outside his immediate neighborhood until 1949, when a feature writer from the *Dallas Morning News* drove out to Williams' cabin in the woods. After this human interest article appeared events moved swiftly, to use a time-honored cliché. Gov. Robert A. Shivers made Williams an honorary colonel. Williams' local paper, the *Texan*, wrote a long and sympathetic piece. The newly-discovered hero was honored at the Franklin courthouse and presented with his colonel's commission and variety of commendations. None of which he could read, a skill he had never mastered, The September 1951 issue of the magazine published by the United Daughters of the Confederacy had him on the cover and many pages of his life inside.

In 1953, *Life* magazine came calling. Williams and his wife posed, unsmiling. The article described their very Spartan existence, the unfinished boards, the tin roof. At his annual birthday barbeque, hundreds of descendants gathered. Now he had more to say about the war. He and his comrades had killed "a hundred Yankees." Grant was about to surrender at Appomattox, if Lee had only held on a little longer. The Air Force honored him, flying Williams to Bergstrom AFB, where he was made honorary base commander for the day, a ceremony presided over by the actor James Stewart. Williams was dressed in a new Confederate uniform, drawn from a Hollywood studio's wardrobe lockers. On his 113th birthday, he was presented with a medal by the Pentagon. Williams was increasingly deaf and weak. But he held on. In 1957 he ran a high fever, but recovered.

In late March 1958, Cooper K. Ragan, soon-to-be head of the Texas Civil War Commission, write to the centenary commission in Washington DC, urging that any ceremony honoring Williams should be held soon, as the old man was fading. In his long report, Ragan noted that no record of military service could be found, but that Williams' receipt of a Texas Confederate pension should suffice at evidence. Meanwhile Colonel Williams had been elevated to the rank of general by the "Sons of the

Confederacy." In June 1959, a group calling itself the Confederate High Command, promoted Williams to five-star general.
This youthful forager now outranked Robert E. Lee. In April 1958
a delegation of long-winded politicians motored out to the little
cabin in the woods, bringing ceremonial documents from the
president, the governor of Texas, and the mayor of Houston.
Cameras flashed. Movie cameras whirred. Williams, nearly deaf
and half-blind, never stirred.

It is likely that he never understood what transpired. He
was no longer a person; he had become a prop. He had become
useful as a symbol of dedicated service and tenacious longevity.
He had become a blank page on which anyone could write their
own political or heritage-inspired agenda.

Williams got older and sicker. And older and sicker.
Everyone wanted part of him. A bevy of politicians leaned on
President Eisenhower to commit to attendance at Williams an-
ticipated funeral. The men commanding Fort Sam Houston in
San Antonio were ordered to prepare for a full military funeral.
A joint resolution of Congress authorized lowering all the na-
tion's flags on the occasion of Williams' death. However, in early
September 1959 a young Washington, DC reporter, Lowell K.
Bridwell, published the results of his deep investigations. His
conclusion: Williams was a fraud. The man's old neighbors re-
called his claims of Civil War soldiering as harmless nonsense.
Even more compelling were the records of the Federal census.

SCHEDULE 1.—Free Inhabitants in _____ in the County of *Itawamba* State of *Miss* *pp* enumerated by me, on the 4ᵗʰ day of *Sept.* 1860. *W H Hison* Asst. Marshal. Post Office *Tremont*

Page No. 321

The 1860 records of Itawamba County, Mississippi, clearly show Walter G. Williams, age five, living with his parents, George and Nancy, and two siblings. Subsequent census findings confirm his age: 1870 (15 years); 1880 (24 years); 1900 (age 46); and 1910 (age 55). However, in the 1930 census, he told the marshal that he was eighty, when in fact he was only seventy-five. This seems to mark a turning point. From here on, Williams added many years to his "age." His motives? We'll never know. (It is interesting to note that in 1880 his occupation was "beef driver," confirming his tales of the Old Chisholm Trail.)

This demotion of Williams, from super-humanly ancient veteran, to much younger fraud did not sit well with his supporters. There was now a vast baggage attached to Williams and his useful symbolism. His daughter Willie Mae described Bridwell's findings as "ridiculous." A past president of the United Daughters of the Confederacy denounced Federal and state records as "incomplete." The national president of the Sons of Confederate Veterans wrote, "There is no doubt in our minds that Williams is a veteran." A senator from Mississippi said that only "overwhelming evidence" of fraud would change the proposed Federal day of mourning. (Logic 101 tells each student that one cannot prove a negative.) The head of the Texas Confederate Pension Fund said, "Those Yankees just think they've killed all of us Confederates off." Price Daniels, governor of Texas, proclaimed "In this matter, we shall respect and follow the records of the state and the Confederacy rather than the archives of the Federal government."

Williams, who never learned of this controversy, continued to grow older and sicker. His body finally gave out December 19, 1959. His elaborate funeral continued as planned. He lay in state, dressed in the gray and gold of a Confederate general as five thousand people trooped by to pay their last respects. Even in death, the doubters didn't get the last word. In 1960, the Texas State legislature passed a long resolution, in which they not only affirmed that secession was a "just and noble act," and that Williams was a proven and valid Confederate veteran, but went on to denounce Bridwell's report as one of the "foulest and most dastardly assaults which only an evil, diseased and venom-filled mind could conceive, less honorably than a rattlesnake—without warning—as the viperous diatribe—the foulest whelp of sin.'" This pox-on-you blast was mild compared with the attack upon *Time* magazine, which was "a strumpet of scandal and a harlot of untruth." These brief excerpts only scratch the surface of the Lone Star State's counter-factual fury.. Copies of the full text, embossed with the great seal of the Republic of Texas, were sent to the governors of every former Confederate state.

Just as the medieval cities fought over holy relics, the bones of the blessed martyrs, whose disarticulated scraps brought honor and prestige to those who held them, the last veterans had become trophies, whose factual identities no longer mattered. We possess them and therefore we possess their stories and the meaning of those stories.

Perhaps, like the institutionalized memories of Karbala, the bitterness of the Civil War will still be with us after the passing of another thirteen centuries.

CHAPTER 7
RECESSIONAL

The tumult and the shouting dies.
The Captains and the Kings depart.
—*Rudyard Kipling*

In an ancient vaudeville routine, Comedian A asks, "How's your wife?" Comedian B responds, "Compared with what?" In a similar vein, this essay has looked at pensions, deserved and undeserved. Can we draw any conclusions? Is there data to even begin such a search? Are there records which would allow us to compare the Confederate experience with the Union experience? Were the different Confederate states different in their generosity toward their Confederate veterans?

In a different sphere, can we enumerate and compare the frequency of misbehavior of different types. Did Union men (per capita) desert more often than Confederate men? And what about alcohol? Can we compare North and South in their drinking patterns? Did different ethnic groups differ in their damaging experiences with strong drink? On both pensions and misbehavior this essay has provided anecdotal evidence, but can we make over-all conclusions? In today's favored jargon can we find Big Data?

Beginning with the subject of the Union pension system, were the applications universally accepted? The 1877 Annual Report of the Secretary of the Interior, covering 1876-1877, gives some answers. In that period, the pension bureau received a total of 23,954 new applications for Army disability pensions. The bureau rejected 4,609—19 percent. The Annual Report was a summary, so the reasons for rejection are not listed, but it is clear that application did not necessarily mean acceptance. Rodgers' review of the 1888 Virginia pension applications indicates that many were rejected, but his summaries did not list the reasons, which would need to be sought in the often incomplete original records. In brief, both North and South, not all applications led to pensions. The exact percentages proved difficult to find.

Another issue in Civil War pensions was the relative generosity of the states and the Federal system. In 1890, at the height of the pension industry, 37 percent of the Federal budget went to veterans' pensions. The *Encyclopedia Virginia* tells us that at its 1908 peak Virginia Civil War pensions constituted 7.3

percent of the state budget, a pale shadow of Union largesse. However, a vital element should not be overlooked. Union pensions went to Union soldiers but taxpayers north <u>and</u> south were funding the Union system. This burden did not go unnoticed by Southern congressmen, none of whom voted in favor of any increase in Union pensions. The South might have had more money for Confederate veterans if they were not already feeding the voracious maw of the GAR.

The pension systems, North and South, were intended for men of loyal service, which excluded deserters. The relative desertion numbers of the two warring sections might shed an oblique light on the virtues, or lack thereof, of the opponents.

The Union armies contained a total of 2,778,304 men. Of these, 337,032 (12 percent) deserted. However, only 10 percent of the deserters were court-martialed. Roughly 300,000 men were gone, no one knew where, and they never came back. The origin of these figures is fully discussed in the author's *Merciful Lincoln* (pages 77 *et seq.*). The thoroughness of these statistics rests upon the work of the Union Provost Marshal General's Bureau, tasked with keeping up-to-date records on every Union deserter. The Confederacy had no such bureau and therefor had no way of knowing how many men had deserted and never returned. Our nearest available source is the microfilmed General Orders of the Army of Northern Virginia (ANVA). These records indicate that the estimated 250,000 men in that army generated 5,970 courts-martial, of which 2,283 were for desertion.

While we have no way of comparing the North and South in regards to the total number of men who ever deserted, we can compare the number of courts-martial for desertion. In the Union armies of 2,778,304 men, 26,014 were tried for desertion—9.3 percent. In the Army of Northern Virginia's 250,000 men, 2,283 were court-martialed for desertion—9.1 percent. To the extent that such figures reflect loyalty to their respective causes, the North and the South were close to identical.

Another frequently used measure of behavior is offences committed while drunk. Sadly, there are no reliable overall figures for the Confederate armies. In the General Orders of the ANVA 3.8 percent of the summaries mention alcohol, but there are no details given. The full-text trial transcripts for the Confederate armies were filed in Richmond. For reasons unknown, the Confederate authorities decided to burn their capital as they departed. Among the incinerated files were those of all the courts-martial.

Up north was a different story. The well-preserved records enable researchers to study many aspects of the war. One was the long-held belief that the Irish troops had more drunkenness. In the author's *Irish & German—Whiskey & Beer* he studied three groups: all the Irish regiments; all the German regiments; and a large sample of "American" regiments, defined as original Yankee stock. Using the mention of alcohol in a court-martial as our measure, we found: Irish (22.4 percent); German (18.0 percent); and American (15.0 percent). The traditional view of Irish drinking was correct.

To return to the principal focus of this essay—pensions —several issues jump out. First, the "tail" of the war, the decades of cost associated with wounds and disease after the war was as great as the war itself during the years 1861-1865. As we have seen in this war and all the other wars since, the ultimate costs are far greater than those predicted by "hawk" politicians and eager generals.

Second, there is no provable evidence of wide-spread pension fraud. Diligent search has turned up a few cases with dramatic—even amusing—aspects, but no actuarial pattern of fraud. Third, the provision of veterans' benefits on a large scale was the beginning of an entitlement society. The author's ancestor who fought in the Revolutionary War received a pension, but pensions from 1776 were small and not issued until most such soldiers were ancient, already knocking on death's door. Today's Social Security, Social Security Disability, Medicaid, Medicare, AFDC, school lunch programs, food stamps, subsidized housing, and Veterans' Hospitals are all the outgrowth of the Civil War pension system. Whether the latter programs are good or bad is not the issue here.

Finally, our very first question—*Was Grandpa a Freeloader?*—now becomes our last question. Grandpa, in this case my great-grandfather, William Henry Simms, Sr., applied for and received a Union pension even though he was wealthy. Under the law he was entitled to this money. It was legal. But was it moral? In enlisting he had taken on all the risks of soldiering: sickness, injury, and death. He has escaped death at Murfreesboro. He had escaped death at Andersonville. He escaped death as the *Sultana* sailed without him. Perhaps his modest check was a late payment for his many close encounters with the Grim Reaper many years before.

His service stands in contrast to the advice given by John D. Rockefeller, Sr. to his younger brother, Frank, when the boy wished to enlist. "You would be a wild foolish boy to go away and waste youthful years that you might utilize in getting a start and making money." (Ron Chernow: *Titan*. Page 70.) Rockefeller and his fellow Robber Barons, such as Andrew Carnegie, J. P. Morgan, and Andrew W. Mellon prospered mightily from the torrent of money unleashed by the war. Even the founder of the author's alma mater, Leland Stanford, did very well in the murky financing of the early railroads. (Stanford did have military service. By being governor he was commander of the California State Militia.)

But is it fair to characterize these titans of industry as robbers? Early left-leaning historians labelled them as such, but a succeeding generation of scholars has rethought this issue and suggested that the designation "Industrial Statesmen" might better suit them. In their monopolies and economic integrations, they brought order and stability into a chaotic economy.

Stepping back from such broad and sweeping issues, was grandpa a freeloader? Not at all. Half a century after the fact, his modest, even symbolic, pension was a very late payment for his risks in battle and prison.

APPENDIX A

THE 1884 PENSION ACT

A Virginia veteran applying for a pension under this law, was given a blank form to complete, with these directions: "The application must be in writing, verified by oath, and must state in what command the applicant served when wounded, when, and where wounded, and the extent of his disability at the time of application, and whether or not he has at any time received any limb, eye or commutation money from any State, or the United States, and if so the nature of the amount of aid received. There must be a certificate of a competent physician in writing, under oath, to the full nature of the wound and extent of the disability of the applicant at the date of application. The [county] clerk must copy the application and certificate of physician, and reduce all the evidence heard in the case to writing and certify the same." Should the applicant wish to review the details of the controlling legislation, the entirety of the law was printed on the back of the application and those words are shown in the following paragraphs. (Since roughly forty percent of Virginia soldiers could not write their own names, it is likely that few read and/or comprehended this material.)

AN ACT TO GIVE AID TO THE CITIZENS OF VIRGINIA, WOUNDED AND MAIMED DURING THAT LATE WAR, WHILE SERVING AS SOLDIERS AND MARINES. APPROVED FEBRUARY 25, 1884.

1.   Be it enacted by the general assembly of Virginia, That the sum of sixty thousand dollars be, and the same is hereby appropriated out of the public treasury, to pay the claims properly allowed upon applications heretofore made under the act of assembly approved February fourteenth, eighteen hundred and eighty-two, entitled an act to provide commutation to such maimed soldiers, sailors, and marines in lieu of artificial limbs, or eyes, otherwise disabled, as may not heretofore have received the same under the provisions of former acts, and, also, the claims which may hereafter be allowed under the provisions of this act. And the auditor of public accounts is hereby authorized to issue his warrants on the treasury, to pay the same to the parties entitled thereto, in the order of time in which they have been and may hereafter be received and filed in his office, provided that the auditor of public accounts shall audit all such

claims in two classes as follows: Class one—Claims of soldiers or marines who have never received any aid from the state, which shall be a preferred class. Class two—Claims of soldiers or marines who have received aid from the state, upon which nothing shall be paid until the claims of the first class shall have been paid, nor, until the first day of June, eighteen hundred and eighty-four, when he shall proceed to pay the claims of the second class.

2.   Any citizen of this state who shall hereafter furnish a certificate from the court of his county or corporation, showing that he is now a citizen of this state, and that during the late war, and while he was a citizen of this state, he was engaged in military service as a soldier, sailor, or marine, and while in such service lost a limb, or eye, or was so seriously and permanently disabled by wounds or surgical operations rendered necessary thereby, as to prevent him at the date of such certificate from performing manual labor, or that while so engaged in such military service he lost a limb or eye, or was so permanently disabled by wounds or surgical operations, and has since loosing [sic] his limb or eye, or being so permanently disabled, remained continuously in this state, and is now a citizen thereof; that he has not at any time received an artificial limb or eye, or commutation money, or pension from any other state or from the United States; and that he has not before the date of his application, received under the provisions of any former act of assembly of this state, an artificial limb, or eye, or commutation money, shall be entitled to the sum of sixty dollars, to be paid as provided in this

act; provided that any such applicant who has heretofore received an artificial limb or commutation therefor, from this state, shall still be entitled to the relief given in this act, if the artificial limb received or purchased with the commutation money received has been worn out or lost, or having lost only one leg has not been able to use an artificial leg, shall be entitled to the sum of sixty dollars; and provided further, that when such applicant has lost both legs or both arms or both eyes , he shall be entitled to the sum of sixty dollars for each limb or eye lost. Before the court shall give such certificate, it shall require the applicant to state in his written application, verified by oath, in what command he was serving when wounded; when, where and how wounded; the nature of the wound and the extent of the disability at that time, and whether or not he has at any time previous received any limb, eye, or commutation money from this state; and if so, the date, nature and amount of the aid so received; and the court shall further require a competent physician to certify in writing, and under oath, the full nature of the wound and the extent of the disability of the applicant at that date, and this certificate of the physician, together with the other evidence in support of the application, given before the court, shall be reduced to writing, and certified, and returned by the clerk, with the application, to the auditor of public accounts.

3.   The auditor shall examine carefully each application, and the certificates and evidence therewith, heretofore returned under the act of February fourteenth, eighteen hundred and eighty-two, and former acts, and which may be returned under

this act, and when a proper case for relief under this act is, in his judgement, made out, he shall issue his warrant on the treasurer to the applicant for the sum of sixty dollars in each case; provided that in any case where the application filed before the passage of this act and the evidence accompanying it, do not enable the auditor to decide upon the merit of the claim, he shall return the same to the applicant, with instructions to renew the same in accordance to the provisions of this act, and the renewed application, when filed within ninety days from the date of the return of the former application, same have the same relative position on the list of applications as the one returned for renewal.

4.   The auditor is directed to enter of record alphabetically in a suitable book, the names of the parties receiving aid under this act, together with the date, nature and amount of any aid heretofore received.

5.   This act shall be in force from its passage.

APPENDIX B

A REAL ONE

Amidst all the fraud, confusion, and difficult documentation, one man stands out: Pleasant Crump. He was truly, verifiably, the last living Confederate veteran. Crump was born in Crawford's Cove, St. Clair County, Alabama on December 23, 1847. His parents were Robert W. Crump and Martha Hathcock Crump. The 1860 census of St. Clair County, Alabama clearly shows Pleasant as age fourteen.

WAS GRANDPA A FREELOADER?

In November 1864 Pleasant left Alabama and at Petersburg, Virginia enlisted in Company A, 10th Alabama Infantry. There were nine Crumps in that regiment: C.C.; Calvin; Israel; James R.; M.B.; P.R.; Reuben D.; Robert G.; and William B. Only one man has a first name beginning a "P." Further, Pleasant often used "Riggs" as a first name. The published stories of Pleasant Crump place him in Company A. However, his few entries in the Compiled Military Service Records place him in Company C.

Confederate.

C *9*[10] **Ala.**

P. R. Crump

Private, Co. ___, 10 *N* Alabama Regiment.

Appears on a

List

of Prisoners of War, belonging to the Army of
Northern Virginia, who have been this day
surrendered by General Robert E. Lee, C. S. A.,
commanding said Army, to Lieut. Genl. U. S.
Grant, commanding Armies of the United States.

Done at Appomattox Court House, Virginia,
April 9, 1865.

List dated *not dated*

Remarks : _____

His military service included the Battle of Hatcher's Run,
the Siege of Petersburg, and Lee's surrender at Appomattox. After the war he settled at Refuge Community, Lincoln, Talladega
County, Alabama, where he served 71 years as a deacon in the
Refuge Baptist Church.

He had five children by his wife Mary Hall. After her death, he married Ella Wallis. The United Confederate Veterans made him an honorary colonel. He died December 31, 1951, having lived a verified 104 years, and is buried in Lincoln's Hall Cemetery.

Pleasant Crump lived more than a century. And what a century! When he first drew breath, it would be another seven years before Commodore Perry opened Japan to the West, another 22 years before the Pope was declared infallible, and another 43 years before the birth of Dwight D. Eisenhower. When Pleasant Crump first opened his eyes, the lower part of Eurasia was ruled by the Ottoman Empire and the Austro-Hungarian Empire. Today's students view Eisenhower as a figure of the distant past, and Talladega hosts a Honda automobile plant employing 4,000 workers.

Pleasant Crump was the real deal, the original merchandise, the genuine article, in actual, provable fact, the last living Confederate soldier.

APPENDIX C
INDEX TO CONFEDERATE REGIMENTS

APPENDIX D

CONFEDERATE VETERAN SCANDAL

A recently discovered three-page pamphlet, dated October 9, 1912, yellowed by age along the margins, tells of fraud, scandal, and political infighting among West Virginia members of the United Confederate Veterans. It's headline title reads *Attention, Confederate Veterans! The Honor of the West Virginia Division is at Stake.*

The local units of the United Confederate Veterans (UCV) were called "camps." Each was named after some honored Confederate leader, and also had a camp number. Charleston, West Virginia had two UCV camps: Robert E. Lee Camp #887 and Robert E. Lee Camp #878. In the pamphlet, Camp 887 accused Camp 878 of allowing "deserters and imposters" to become members and of listing dead veterans as current members. Further, Camp 887 accused Camp 878 are listing 887 members as 878 members. Why would anybody care? There were at least three reasons.

First, having more members gave clout in voting during UCV conventions. Second, UCV by-laws required proof of "honorable service" which many members did not have. Third, some UCV members applied for state pensions, citing their UCV membership as proof of "honorable service."

The camp members who wrote this complaint included five men whose service can be confirmed: James Z. McChesney (11th Va. Cav.); W. H. Cackley (19th Va. Cav.); Simpson Ellis (45th Va. Inf. Bn.); A. C. L. Gatewood (11th Va. Cav.); Nathaniel O. Sowers (2nd Va. Inf.); and A. P. Pence (Lowry's Battery). Four other men's identity could not be confirmed. Two dead men counted as members of the UCV were James R. Groves (59th Va. Inf.), who died in 1912, and Philip Holesapple (26th Va. Inf. Bn.) who died in 1910.

Long-time students of these records estimate that by the late 1920s every West Virginia Confederate pensioner or "veteran" was an impostor. This poses some real questions for today's members of the Sons of Confederate Veterans and their claims upon history.

SOURCES

Library of Virginia. Digitized Virginia Veteran Pension Applications.

Fold3.com. Digitized Confederate Service Records.

Fold3.com. Digitized Union Service Records.

Abraham Lincoln Presidential Library. Grand Army of the Republic Records.

Ancestry.com. Digitized Illinois Probate Records.

Serrano, Richard A.: *Last of the Blue and Gray.* Smithsonian Books. Washington, DC. 2013.

Rodgers, Mark, E.: *Tracing the Civil War Veteran Pension System in the State of Virginia.* The Edwin Mellen Press. Queenston, Ontario. 1999.

INDEX

Idle
Winter
Press